リーダーをめざす貴女へ
Discover the Aspiring Leader In You

~Bringing the People Deal to Life~

シスコシステムズ合同会社
Project Quantum 事務局 編

ダイヤモンド社

すべての女性たち──ワーキング マザー、働き始めたばか
りの女性、家にいてもオフィスにいても活躍する女性、リー
ダーを目指すあらゆる職業の女性、そしてリーダーを目指す
貴女にこの本を捧げます。

We dedicate this book to all women. To the working
mothers, to the women starting their careers, to the women at
home and the women at the workplace, to the aspiring leaders
in all walks of life… to the aspiring leader in you.

"If you want to awaken all of humanity, then awaken all of yourself. If you want to eliminate the suffering in the world, then eliminate all that is dark and negative in yourself. Truly, the greatest gift you have to give is that of your own self-transformation."

—— Lao Tsu 『Tao Te Ching』

マインドを変えれば
キャリアが変わる

"Project Quantum" をサポートして

内永ゆか子（うちなが・ゆかこ）
NPO法人J-Win理事長
株式会社GRI社長
東京大学理学部物理学科卒。1971年日本IBM入社、取締役専務執行役員をもって退職。NPO法人J-Winを立ち上げ理事長に就任し現在に至る。その間にベネッセホールディングス取締役副社長、ベルリッツコーポレーション代表取締役会長兼社長兼CEOも歴任。

Project Quantum 始動

　シスコはネットワーク分野における世界的なリーダーです。シリコンバレーの本社では本当に多種多様な人たちが働いていますが、それに比べると日本法人の多様性は不十分といわざるをえません。同じような課題を、多くの外資系企業の日本法人が抱えています。

　NPO法人J-Winは2007年の設立以来、企業におけるダイバーシティ・マネジメントの促進と定着を目指し、各種活動を行ってまいりました。業種や業態の枠を超えた女性企業人の相互研鑽の機会を提供し、ネットワーキングの構築を支援することにより、女性リーダーの育成、能力開発を図っています。またGRI

では、企業の実情に即してより実践的なアドバイスができるよう、コンサルティングなどを行っています。

　Project Quantumのターゲットは女性です。日本法人で働く女性たちがこれまで以上に活躍し、リーダーとして成長するために何をすべきか——。私たちはシスコの幹部やプロジェクト事務局と議論をしながら、Project Quantumをサポートしました。

ジョブ・ディスクリプション、業務プロセス、テレワーク

　女性がいきいきと仕事をする職場、女性リーダーを輩出する職場をつくる上で、重要なポイントがいくつかあります。組織や制度を含めた「職場環境」と、「個人の意識」の両面から考えてみましょう。

　女性が働きやすい職場環境の土台として、私はジョブ・ディスクリプションを極めて重要な要素だと考えています。個々人の業務領域や責任範囲が明確であること、自分が何によって評価されるのかという評価基準が明示されているかどうかは、働き方やモチベーションに大きな影響を与えます。

　逆に自分の役割や評価があいまいな環境では、仕事を自分でマネージするのは難しく、夜遅くまで残業を強いられることも多くなるでしょう。とりわけ育児中の女性にとって、働きやすい職場とはいえません。

　もう1つの要素が、時間と場所にとらわれずに仕事のできる環境です。ITシステムの進化は、女性にとって追い風です。自

宅など職場以外の場所でも効率よく働ける環境が整ってきたことで、だからこそ仕事を続けられるという女性も増えています。

テレワークのための様々な道具はシスコの商品であり、当然、社内のテレワーク環境も整備されています。また、明確な業務プロセスと情報システムがあるので、自宅で仕事をしていても「次に何をすればいいのか」を正確に理解することができます。

業務プロセスが可視化されていない企業では、「次に何をすべきか」も明示されません。チームのみんなが集まって長々と話し合い、何となくコンセンサスができあがるということが多いのではないでしょうか。これでは、テレワーク環境があっても有効に活用されないでしょう。

シスコにはジョブ・ディスクリプションがあり、テレワーク環境や明確な業務プロセスがあります。多くの日本企業の現状と比較すれば、働き続けたいと考えている女性にとって恵まれた環境です。

ロールモデルをつくり、増やす

次に個人のレベルでは、ロールモデルとマインドセットがキーワードです。

日本におけるシスコの課題は、キャリアアップを目指す女性、つまり Project Quantum の参加メンバーにとってのロールモデルが社内にあまり見当たらないことでした。身近なところにロールモデルとなる女性がいれば、今後のキャリア形成について具体的にイメージすることができます。親しくなれば、メンター

として話を聞いてもらうこともできるでしょう。

今回のプロジェクトは、参加メンバーたちとダイバーシティの意味を考えることからスタートしました。例えば、企業がダイバーシティ・マネジメントに取り組む理由、個々の女性にとっての意味などについて深く理解してもらう必要があります。

加えて、個別の面談も行いました。私は彼女たち一人ひとりとじっくり話し合いました。一種のメンタリングです。仕事上の相談はもちろん、個人的な悩みなど、ふだんは胸にしまっているようなことも語ってもらいました。

この面談をはじめ各種の施策の中で、最も重視したのは『マインドを変える』ことです。当初の印象を率直にいうと、「絶対にキャリアアップする」という気持ちを持った参加メンバーは少なかったと思います。自信が足りないとも感じました。

問題を乗り越えていく、という強い気持ちを持つ

マインドを変えるためのカギは、足元の問題に気をとられるのではなく、前を見るということです。

一人ひとりが大なり小なり、何らかの問題を抱えています。それらの問題ばかりを気にしていては、前に進むことはできません。1つの問題を解けば、必ず次の問題が現れます。キリがありません。重要なのは問題を解決することよりも、問題があっても乗り越えていこうとする強い気持ちを持つことです。

人は往々にして、解決の難しい問題をエクスキューズの材料にします。「だからしょうがない」と、自分を納得させてしまう

のです。それは恐ろしいことです。

　面談の中でもその種の話を聞きました。「育児があるから」とか「家の事情があるから」とか。そんなとき私は、「障害を、自分がやらない言い訳にしないこと」といいます。世界を見渡せばもっと大きな困難を抱えながら、がんばって成果をあげている人もたくさんいるのです。

　「ここには、恵まれた職場環境がある。あなたたちは期待されているし、チャンスを与えられている。スキルもある。それなのに、なぜチャレンジしないのか」。そういって背中を押しながら、キャリアアップの先にある楽しさや素晴らしいことを具体的にイメージしてもらいました。

　Project Quantumは参加メンバーのマインドに影響を与えたと思います。面談をしているとき、私のちょっとした一言で表情が変わった女性が多くいました。その表情の奥には、ポジティブな変化が感じられました。

　プロジェクトに参加した女性たちには、今後、シスコにおいてロールモデルとしての役割を担うことが期待されています。すでに、若手の女性たちからはロールモデル、またはそれに近い存在として見られていることでしょう。この経験を生かして参加メンバーの多くが、やがて本物のロールモデルへと成長してくれると私は信じています。

A change in attitude can change your career

Support for Project Quantum

Yukako Uchinaga
J-Win (NPO) Board Chair and
President of the Global Research Institute (GRI)

Ms. Uchinaga graduated from the Department of Physics in the University of Tokyo's Faculty of Science. She entered IBM in 1971 and retired from the company as Japan IBM, Board of Director and Vice President, General Manager of Asia Pacific Development Organizations. In 2007, she founded the NPO J-Win, assuming the position of Chairman of the Board. In 2008, she became Executive Vice President of Benesse Holdings, Inc., and simultaneously Berlitz Corporation's Chairman of the Board, Chief Executive Officer, and President.

Project Quantum Launch

Cisco Systems is a global leader in the field of networks. Though a great variety of individuals work at the corporate headquarters in Silicon Valley, one must say that diversity is absent at the corporate office in Japan. Many foreign-owned enterprises in Japan face the same issue.

Since J-Win was founded in 2007, we have sought the promotion and integration of corporate diversity management through varied means. We have helped businesswomen across industries and categories find opportunities for reciprocal study and supported network building opportunities, fostering of female leaders and development of potential. GRI (the Global Research Institute), meanwhile, provides practical advice through consulting and other services tailored to individual corporations' circumstances.

Project Quantum is aimed at women. Its goal is to help corporate women in Japan become more active, and to identify steps required to help female leaders enjoy personal growth. We conducted discussions with Cisco Systems management and the Secretariat in our effort to support Project Quantum.

Job description, business processes, and telework

There are salient points to consider aside from workplaces where women can thrive and the nurturing of female leaders. We must give consideration to the dual issues of work environment-- including organizations and systems--and individual awareness.

I believe that job description is an exceedingly important component of the fundamental work environment for women. Motivation and how one approaches work are influenced by how specifically one's sphere of work and duties are clarified, and the standards by which one will be evaluated.

Put differently, if one's role and assessment remain vague, self-management of work is difficult, often enhancing pressure to invest long overtime hours. That certainly does not describe a work-friendly environment, particularly for women during the childrearing years.

Another factor is whether the environment is work-friendly, regardless of time or place. IT systems have evolved favorably for women, who can now work efficiently at home and elsewhere outside the office, allowing more women to continue working.

Cisco Systems produces a number of devices used in telework, and of course telework environments also exist within the company. And as business processes and information systems are elucidated, one can work at home with a clear understanding of which task to do next.

Those tasks remain unclear in companies with no visualized business process. In such cases, teams probably gather, debate at length, and eventually arrive at a consensus. Telework environments cannot be effective in such climates.

Cisco Systems offers well-clarified job descriptions, telework environments, and clear business processes. It offers women who wish to continue working a more favorable environment than that provided by most other Japanese enterprises at the moment.

Role models: create and proliferate

Next, on the individual level, "role model" and "mind-set" are the key words to remember.

Cisco Systems in Japan faced the challenge of few in-house role models for the participants of Project Quantum, who were women eager for corporate advancement. When such role models exist close at hand, they afford women a clear image of how their own careers might unfold. Such situations also give female mentors a chance to voice their experiences.

This time, Project Quantum began with a chance for

participants to consider the meaning of diversity. One topic was the necessity for a deep understanding of what significance a company's reason for incorporating diversity management would have for each female employee.

The project also involved individual interviews. I spoke at length with each female participant. That was also a form of mentoring. The women confided their work-related questions, of course, but also their private worries and issues which normally remained trapped within their minds.

Many measures were discussed during the interviews, but "changing your attitude" was the one given the most importance. To be honest, my first impression was that few of the women were absolutely committed to advancing in their career. I had the feeling that many lacked confidence.

A determination to overcome obstacles

The key to changing one's attitude is directing one's focus ahead instead of being distracted by immediate problems.

Each of us has problems, be they large or small. If we focus exclusively on these problems, we cannot progress. Solving one problem simply illuminates the next one lying in wait. It is an endless process. Solving a given problem is not of utmost importance--being driven by a determination to overcome issues, on the other hand, is.

People sometimes use a particularly thorny issue as an excuse to write off progress and convince themselves that there is no hope. That is a dangerous road to tread.

In fact, I heard such arguments during my interviews. Participants cited childrearing or family issues as excuses. I always respond by advising individuals not to use such obstacles as overriding excuses. I point out that many people in the world around us have faced much greater hindrances and yet have enjoyed success.

"Cisco Systems has a truly favorable working environment," I pointed out to the Project Quantum women. "The company is rooting for you, and you have been given a chance. You have skills. Why, then, do you not seize the opportunity?" With that nudge, I tried to illustrate the joys and wonders of advancing in one's career, leaving participants with a clear image.

I think I had some influence on participants. Many women's expressions transformed during the interview after hearing a few words from me. I felt a positive change unfolding behind that transformed expression.

The hope is that Project Quantum participants will themselves become role models. Younger women in the company no doubt already view them as such, or as colleagues to be respected. I fully believe that the participants will put their Project Quantum experience to work, and will soon evolve into fully-fledged role models.

目次

マインドを変えればキャリアが変わる·············6
"Project Quantum" をサポートして
内永ゆか子
NPO 法人 J-Win 理事長
株式会社 GRI 社長

A change in attitude can change your career···············11
Support for Project Quantum
Yukako Uchinaga
J-Win (NPO) Board Chair and
President of the Global Research Institute (GRI)

———— はじめに Introduction ————

情熱、学習、勇気··············20
フランシーヌ カツォーダス
Senior Vice President, Chief People Officer, Cisco

Passion. Learning. Courage.··············24
Francine Katsoudas
Senior Vice President, Chief People Officer, Cisco

リーダーシップのインスピレーションと
コラボレーションの力··············28
シャリー スレート
Vice President, Chief Inclusion and Collaboration Officer, Cisco

Leadership Inspiration and
the Power of Collaboration··············30
Shari Slate
Vice President, Chief Inclusion and Collaboration Officer, Cisco

もし限界というものがなければ、
あなたは何をしますか？　また、
その行動のスタート地点はどこにしますか？··············32
ジャネット レイミー
Vice President, Cisco Technical Services Asia Pacific, Japan and Greater China

What would you do
if there were no limitations?
And where would you start?··············34
Janet Ramey
Vice President, Cisco Technical Services Asia Pacific, Japan and Greater China

Contents

シスコが進める
「インクルージョン&コラボレーション」とは ································36
What is "Inclusion & Collaboration"?
Project Quantum 事務局

女性リーダー育成プログラム Project Quantum··············46
Project Quantum：Fostering female leaders
Project Quantum 事務局

第1章 /Chapter 1 ··· 57
チャレンジ /Challenge

第2章 /Chapter 2 ··· 89
コミュニケーション /Communication
ネットワーキング /Networking

第3章 /Chapter 3 ·· 115
影響力 /Influence
ダイバーシティ /Diversity

第4章 /Chapter 4 ·· 135
自己認識 /Self-recognition

第5章 /Chapter 5 ·· 161
自信 /Confidence
セルフ ブランディング /Self-branding
チャンスをつかむ /Get a chance

CISCOの女性リーダー❶
コンフォートゾーンを飛び出す
一瞬の躊躇はあっても、挑戦する ·· 186
佐藤菜穂子

Cisco Women Leaders
Jump out of your comfort zone
Even if you have a momentary hesitation,
take the challenge. ·· 190
Naoko Sato

CISCOの女性リーダー❷
エンジニアからの方向転換、
自分に何ができるかを考えた ·· 194
山田晴香

Cisco Women Leaders
When I took a step away from engineering,
I wondered what my capabilities were. ················· 198
Haruka Yamada

エピローグ ·· 202
アネラ ハイテン
Vice President, Human Resources APJC, Cisco

Epilogue ·· 205
Annella Heytens
Vice President, Human Resources APJC, Cisco

おわりに ·· 208
Final message

Project Quantum 第一期メンバー プロフィール ················· 212
Project Quantum Member Profile

はじめに

Introduction

Francine Katsoudas
フランシーヌ カツォーダス

Senior Vice President,
Chief People Officer
Cisco

情熱、学習、勇気

　これらはシスコを特徴づける言葉のほんの一部ですが、素晴らしい社員と、これまで築き上げてきた私たちの企業文化をよく表しています。この本では、これらの言葉が意味することをより深く理解し、日本の卓越した女性リーダーたちからユニークな洞察を得ることができるでしょう。彼女たちは、自身のキャリア デベロップメントの一部として、新しいことに挑戦し、スキルを伸ばすために Project Quantum というプログラムに参加する機会を得ました。1年間の学びを終えた彼女たちの洞察に富むメッセージを読めば、あなたの中のリーダーシップが目を覚まし、自身に対する関心が湧き起こることでしょう。あるいは、潜在能力を開花させるために積極的に行動し、ブレークスルーを成し遂げたいという思いに駆り立てられるかもしれません。

　私個人としても、これまでのキャリアの中で、恐れを知らない女性たちから影響や導きを受けたことを幸運に感じています。自分の限界を超え、好奇心を持ち、リスクを負い、情熱を持つ

て行動し、そして「今日は何を学べただろうか」「どんな影響を
与えられただろうか」と自問するように背中を押してもらいまし
た。新たなチャンスを探し、失敗から学び、最高のメンターに
恵まれたことによって、私は社員としてより成長し、リーダー
となることができました。私はシスコのリーダーとして、社員
が自分のキャリアを築いてゆく過程において、有意義かつ革新
的な体験をしてほしいと願っています。

　シスコは人に重きを置くことでリーダーシップを発展させ、
多様な才能あふれる人材が長期的に活躍できる環境を提供し続
けています。こうした取り組みのすべてが、シスコのビジネス
上の戦略をサポートするために活用されているのです。

　シスコの People Deal は、社員一人ひとりが潜在能力を解き
放ち、真の自分らしさを発揮できるようにするためのものです。
どうすればすべてがコネクションし、あらゆる分野で革新が起
こり、すべての社員にとって有益になるかということに焦点を
当てています。

Francine Katsoudas
フランシーヌ カツォーダス

Senior Vice President,
Chief People Officer
Cisco

・シスコは、人、プロセス、データ、モノ、それらすべてをつなぐことで、世界をより良いものにしたいと考えています。夢を夢だけでは終わらせません。日々それを実現させています。

・シスコは、あらゆる分野で変革を起こし、斬新なアイディアと可能性を生み出しています。恐れずにリスクを負い、未来を創造します。失敗から学ぶことさえできれば、すべての失敗は成功となることを知っているからです。

・シスコは、社員やお客様、そして世界の人々のために意義のある変化を起こします。全員が喜びを共有できるような成功を導くために、相互に助け合い、ともに実行します。

　私たちは、一体感のあるコラボレーション環境をつくり出し、革新的なことを生み出すためのコミットメントを共有することで、社員の潜在能力を引き出そうと努めています。女性が権限を持って活躍することは、シスコの成功や継続的な成長のために欠かせません。多様な視点を有することは、優れた会社であ

るという証です。私たちの究極の目標は、社員、お客様、パートナー企業の一人ひとりに、シスコから歓迎され、敬意を払われ、その声に耳を傾けるべき大切な存在だと認められている、と感じてもらうことです。

　この本を読めば、彼女たちが学びや情熱、新たな視点を身につけたいという願望を常に抱いていることがわかると思います。そして、その願望は読んでいるみなさんにも伝わるでしょう。

　人生は、自分が思い描く未来に向けて築いていくことができる。そのことを彼女たちは思い起こさせてくれます。自分が歩む道筋さえわかっていれば、その道は必ず開けると私は信じています。大切なのは「正しい」道筋ではなく、「自分の」道筋を見つけることなのです。

　この本に登場する女性たちが語る内容や成し遂げたことに、きっと強く感銘することでしょう。ぜひ楽しながら読み、そして何かを考え、学び取ってください。

Francine Katsoudas

Senior Vice President,
Chief People Officer
Cisco

Passion. Learning. Courage.

These are just a few words that describe Cisco, our amazing
people and the strong culture we have built together. In this book,
you will read more about what these words mean and gain unique
insight from a group of incredible female leaders in Japan who
embraced the opportunity to spend a year to learn, experiment
and broaden their skills as part of their career journeys. Their
insightful messages will awaken the leader in you, inspire you to be
more self-aware, drive you to make bold choices and encourage
you to explore and discover your own breakthroughs to fulfill
your potential.

Personally, I am so fortunate to have been influenced and
guided by fearless women in my life who inspired me to push
beyond my boundaries, to be curious, to take risks, to follow my
passion and always ask myself "What did I learn today?" and
"What is my impact?" Having the ability to explore new

opportunities, to embrace learnings from failure, to have the best mentors — this is what made me a better employee and people leader. And as a leader, I want to enable the most positive and innovative experience for all of our employees as they architect their own paths.

With an intense focus on our people, we are growing and developing leadership, attracting and retaining the most diverse talent and aligning all of these efforts to support our business strategy.

Our People Deal is about unleashing every employee's potential so they can be their authentic selves. It focuses on how we connect everything, innovate everywhere and benefit everyone.

— We connect everything – people, process, data and things — and we use those connections to change our world for the better. We don't just dream it, we do it every day.

25•

Francine Katsoudas

Senior Vice President,
Chief People Officer
Cisco

— We innovate everywhere to create fresh ideas and possibilities. Taking bold risks to shape the future because we understand every failure is a success if we learn from it.

— We make a meaningful difference for our people, our customers and the world around us. We support each other and work together to create shared success that will benefit everyone.

We strive to bring out everyone's potential by driving an inclusive and collaborative environment and collectively sharing a commitment to make amazing things happen. Empowering women at Cisco is an incredibly important part of our success and continued growth. We are a better company if we have diverse perspectives, and ultimately our goal is to ensure that every single employee, customer and partner feels welcomed, valued, respected and heard.

As you read about the experiences of these women you will see their relentless hunger for learning, passion and perspective. And it is contagious.

They also remind us that we have the opportunity to build our own future, based on the future we can envision. My belief is that if you know what your path is, you can bring that path to you. And it is not about the "right" path, but the "you" path.

The voices and realizations of the women in this book can be a powerful inspiration to all of us. Enjoy reading, reflecting and learning!

Shari Slate
シャリー スレート

Vice President,
Chief Inclusion and
Collaboration Officer
Cisco

リーダーシップのインスピレーションとコラボレーションの力

　シスコ社内、またお客様やパートナー企業間における多様性、一体化、コラボレーションにまつわる会話は変化しつつあります。全社員が潜在能力を真に発揮すべき新時代の幕開けです。私はシスコのチーフ インクルージョン アンド コラボレーション オフィサーとして、革新的なアイデアや新鮮なアプローチ、進取果敢な行動、そして何よりも情熱を持って変化を起こし続けるリーダーの方々と会話ができることを光栄に思います。

　私たちの潜在能力を存分に引き出し、飛躍を遂げるための原動力となるものは、やはり情熱です。本書はそのような情熱にあふれています。その名のとおり画期的な Project Quantum の参加者たちから得た深い洞察をまとめ、個人としての飛躍を遂げた 13 名の女性たちに光を当てています。

　ぜひ、じっくりと読んでみてください。そして、この本から

得た見識をあなた自身の成長やあなたの組織にどのように活用
できるかを考えてほしいと思います。これは女性によってつく
られた本ですが、彼女たちの物事の本質を見抜くスキルは、文
化や性別、民族、社会的立場、能力、背景、経験、ワークスタ
イル、ものの見方といった、いかなる違いをも乗り越える力を
持っているのです。

　この素晴らしい本を読むことで、シスコの People Deal に命
が吹き込まれるのを、私は身をもって実感しました。本書は多
くの人に共有されるべき作品です。読めばきっと、飛躍を目指
す人にすすめたり、ツイートで広めたり、誰かと話題にしたく
なったりすることでしょう。

Shari Slate

Vice President,
Chief Inclusion and
Collaboration Officer
Cisco

Leadership Inspiration and the Power of Collaboration

All across Cisco, and across our customers and partners the conversation around diversity, inclusion, and collaboration is reaching an inflection point. We are witnessing the beginning of a new era in which we truly unleash the power and potential of our people. As Cisco's Chief Inclusion and Collaboration Officer, I am privileged to spend my days talking to the people who are making that happen through innovative ideas, fresh new approaches, bold action, and most of all passion.

It is passion first and foremost that will enable us to "take the leap" and to realize our full potential. Discover the Aspiring Leader In You, Bringing the People Deal to Life is full of such passion. A collection of insights from participants in the groundbreaking and aptly named Project Quantum, it shines with the light of those 13 women who have made their own personal

●30

leap.

I urge you to read this book slowly, contemplating how you can put each insight to work within your development and across your organization. While it was written by women, each insight applies to the full spectrum of diversity - cultures, gender, ethnicities, affiliations, abilities, backgrounds, experiences, work styles, and points-of-view.

In reading this delightful book, I truly did experience Cisco's People Deal brought to life. This is a work created to share. Read it and I guarantee you will want to share a copy, share a tweet, or share a conversation with somebody else ready to take "the leap".

Janet Ramey
ジャネット レイミー

Vice President,
Cisco Technical Services Asia Pacific,
Japan and Greater China

もし限界というものがなければ、
あなたは何をしますか？ また、
その行動のスタート地点はどこにしますか？

　掲題は、この本全体を通して静かに読者に投げかけられる質問です。コミュニケーションやネットワークづくりの方法、自分のブランドをつくりだして成果を認めてもらう方法、効果的に人の心を動かす方法などのヒントを探しているのであれば、この本から実用的なヒントを得ることができます。また、この本では、ヒントをあげるだけでなく、より高い目標を設定して自分自身を信じることを強く勧めています。

　この本の素晴らしいところは、アドバイスが控えめであくまで個人の一意見としている点です。注意深く耳を傾ければ、経験と希望に満ちた声が聞こえてくるでしょう。この本に登場する女性たちは、互いに切磋琢磨し、学んだ教訓を身につけ、リーダーとしてのキャリアを歩みながら学び続ける姿を通じて、読者に直接語りかけてきます。シンプルで力強いアドバイスは、

勇気とインスピレーションを与えてくれます。

　俳優のスティーヴ・マーティンは、かつてこう言いました。「無視できないくらい、うまくなれ」。私の好きな言葉です。このわかりやすさは心に訴えるものがあります。そして、経験上、この言葉は真実です。「うまく」仕事をしましょう。認められるためには、まずは優れた成果をあげる必要があります。そうすれば、信頼を築き、自分自身の力を見出し、自分の中にあるリーダーとしての素質を引き出すことが可能になります。

　この本を読み終わったら、感想を友人や会社の同僚、お姉さんや妹さん、娘さん、お母様と話し合ってみてください。これをきっかけに、読者の皆様が自信を築き、大胆な目標の達成に向けた道を思い切って歩み出されることを願っています。

Janet Ramey

Vice President,
Cisco Technical Services Asia Pacific,
Japan and Greater China

What would you do if there were no limitations? And where would you start?

Those questions run like an undercurrent through this book.
Whether you're looking for tips on communication and
networking, how to manage your brand and be recognized for
your achievements, or how to influence effectively, this book
provides you with practical tips. But more than tips, this book
exhorts you to aim higher and believe in yourself.

What I love about this book is the humble and personal advice.
If you listen carefully, you can hear the voices of both experience
and hope. These women speak directly to you, as they encourage
each other and remind themselves of the lessons they've learned
and keeping learning on their leadership journeys. I am
encouraged and inspired by the simple yet powerful
recommendations.

Steve Martin, the actor, once said "Be so good they can't ignore you." I love that quote – it's simplicity appeals to me and in my experience, it's true. Be very good at your job; your outstanding performance is the basis for being recognized, which enables you to build confidence, discover your power, and uncover the leader within you.

Enjoy this book, and share it with your friends and colleagues, your sisters, daughters, mothers. May it inspire you to have confidence, take a risk and set a path to achieve your bold goals.

シスコが進める
「インクルージョン＆コラボレーション」とは

ダイバーシティを前提とした
「インクルージョン＆コラボレーション」への取り組み

　シスコでは創業時からインクルージョン＆ダイバーシティ（I&D）という名のもと、多様な人材の活用およびお互いを受容する文化の浸透を進めてきました。そして数年前から、ダイバーシティ、インクルージョン、コラボレーションそしてテクノロジーがもたらすビジネス価値の創造について、社内外の有識者との会話を重ね、調査を続けてきました。2014年夏、ナンバーワンITカンパニーを目指すというシスコのビジョンのもと、数年間の調査で培った新しいアイデアや革新的な取り組みを実践するため、名称をインクルージョン＆コラボレーション（I&C）へと変更しました。

　I&Cへの進化は、社員の意識改革を促し、ビジネス価値の創造を目指すことをより明確化していくために必要不可欠です。また、ダイバーシティ（多様な人材の活躍）にも継続して注力していきます。データが情報の一部であるように、シスコではダイバーシティはすでにインクルージョンの一部に組み込まれています。ダイバーシティを前提とし、多様な社員がどうお互いに意見やアイデアを出し合い、自身の業務に活かしていくのか、その点に注力する活動を全社で推進しています。

36

具体的な取り組みや工夫

2011年にI&C専任マネージャーを任命すると同時に、部門横断的なI&Cリーダーシップ チームを設置しました（当時はI&Dと呼んでいました）。リーダーシップ チームは全社的な戦略策定と実行、進捗管理、各部門への意識づけと行動変革の促進を担っています。

また、社内でアンバサダーと呼ぶ推進役のボランティアを募集し、リーダーシップ チームの助言を得ながら、ボトムアップで社員の創意を活かした自主的な活動を展開しています。アンバサダーには女性、男性、外国人、障がい者など多様な人材が参画しています。全社的に I&C を啓蒙し、定着させるため、毎年I&C週間を開催して外部スピーカーの講演、重点テーマの活動報告やテレワークの推奨などを行っています。

●

シスコでは、I&C推進にあたり、カルチャー、プロセス、テクノロジーの3つを必要不可欠な要素として定義し、社員が時間や場所を問わずコラボレーションできるようにテレワーク環境を整えています。

まずは、社員がチームとして自律的にコラボレーションを進める一番の前提となる、共通の価値観（カルチャー）の浸透が求められます。シスコでは社員全員が体現すべき価値観をシスコ

カルチャーと呼んでいます。さらに部門ごとのワークショップで徹底した議論を行うことを通して、社員一人ひとりの深い理解を促進してきました。

次にビジネス プロセスです。社員がテレワーク環境を遠慮なく安心して常時活用するには、社員一人ひとりの役割と目標を明確化し、成果を正当に評価する仕組みの確立が不可欠です。個々の社員は会社の戦略に沿って、目標管理によって優先業務や達成目標を設定、合意します。また、所属長と部下が 目標管理に基づいて進捗管理、中間評価、改善指導のための対話を行うことで、業績評価の透明性を確保しています。

また、社員の参画度 (Engagement) を高めるために、成果の認知 (Recognition) を重視しており、素晴らしい仕事をお互いに讃え合う仕組みとして Connected Recognition という褒賞制度もあります。社員間でいつでも誰からでも成果を認め合えるこの制度により、I&C ボランティア グループの活動をはじめ、社員が部門を超えたコラボレーションに意欲的に取り組む動機づけともなっています。

最後にテクノロジーです。シスコは社員がテレワークを効果的、効率的に行えるように、常に最新のIT設備、ネットワーク機器を導入し、全社展開しています。ビデオ会議システム、Web会議システム、ビジネス チャットやコミュニケーション ツールなどを状況に応じて使い分けることができ、いつでも瞬時に

必要な社員とコミュニケーションできます。すべての社員がPC
を活用することはもとより、現在はBYOD（Bring Your Own
Device）という考え方で、スマートフォンやタブレット端末など
あらゆるデバイスがセキュアなモバイル環境で利用可能となっ
ています。

　このような全社をあげた取り組みが評価され、2015年2月に
公益財団法人日本生産性本部よりエンパワーメント大賞優秀賞
を受賞しました。経営戦略としてインクルージョン＆コラボレー
ションに取り組み、「異文化の受容」「女性活躍の推進」「柔軟な
働き方」の3つを重要テーマとして強力に推進していること、テ
レワークを活用したワークスタイル変革を実施していること、
部門横断的なI&Cリーダーシップ チームを設置し、全社的に社
員への意識づけと行動変革を促進する推進体制を整備している
ことなどが高く評価されました。

インクルージョン&コラボレーションへの進化
Transformational Shift to Inclusion & Collaboration

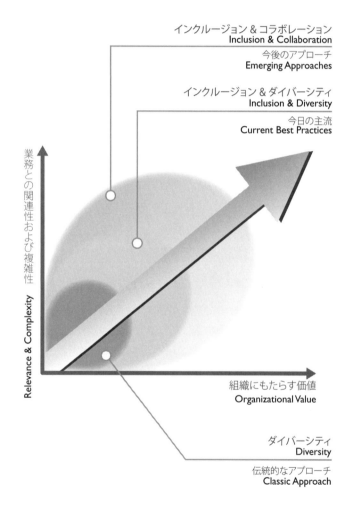

What is "Inclusion & Collaboration"?

Inclusion and Collaboration is an innovative, value-driven model designed to identify the key drivers of highly inclusive, collaborative organizations.

Inclusion has long been both a core value and a deep commitment for Cisco. For the past four years we have been driving thought leadership and cutting edge research, exploring intriguing theories on the business value created through the convergence of diversity, inclusion, collaboration, and technology. In 2014 we decided to make a shift – leveraging these bold new ideas and a transformational approach to accelerate the drive to become the world's number one IT company.

Why the change to Inclusion and Collaboration – what happened to Diversity? The change is critical to shifting mindsets, makes our value clear, and differentiates the transformational work of identifying the key drivers of highly inclusive, collaborative organizations from the classic approach to Inclusion and Diversity. Diversity is built into Inclusion – it's foundational to our work in the same way that data is foundational to information. We are shifting the focus to the true value we are creating.

Inclusion & Collaboration at Cisco Japan

In 2011, a dedicated I&C manager was appointed in Japan, and a cross-functional I&C leadership team was established concurrently. This Inclusion leadership team(ILT) is responsible for setting company-wide strategy and executing as well as enhancing awareness and promoting behavior changes in each representative organization.

Further, volunteer promoters, also referred to as ambassadors, are being recruited within the company, and voluntary activities are being introduced which leverage the creativity of employees from the bottom-up while receiving guidance from the ILT team. A variety of employees, including females, males, foreigners, people with disabilities, etc., are participating as ambassadors. There are three groups; 1) Cross Cultural Connection, 2) Connected Women and 3) Flexible Work Practice. One of the key activities which ambassadors have been driving is an annual I&C Week to promote the awareness of I&C. Through the week, we have key note speeches by external speakers, panel discussions, tele-working day, etc.

For I&C promotions at Cisco Japan, the 3 elements of culture, process and technology are defined as essential elements.

Culture

First, propagation of common values is required, which is the most important factor for employees to autonomously promote team collaboration. The values that all employees at Cisco should embody have been defined as "Cisco Culture". This booklet has been distributed to all employees. Additionally, a deep understanding of individual employees has been promoted through discussions in workshops in each organization.

Process

Establishing a structure in which the roles and goals of each employee are defined and their achievements are evaluated properly is essential for employees to be able to consistently use the telework environment with ease and without hesitation. Individual employees agree on priority tasks and set their job goals linked to company strategy. Also, leaders and employees ensure the transparency of performance review through interactions regarding progress management, short/long term career discussion and coaching.

Further, in order to increase the engagement of employees, there is a focus on recognition of achievements, and there is also a reward system known as Connected Recognition that serves as a mechanism for mutual praise for a job well done. This system of mutual recognition of achievements by anyone at any time between employees has also become a motivation for employees to eagerly make efforts towards collaboration beyond departments, including in the activities of the I&C volunteer group.

Technology

In order to allow employees to carry out telework effectively and efficiently, Cisco is continually introducing and deploying the latest IT facilities and network equipment company-wide. Video-conferencing systems, web meeting systems, business chat and communication tools, etc., can be used depending on the situation, and communication with any required employee is possible on-demand. All employees naturally use PCs, and the current approach is BYOD (Bring Your Own Device). All devices, such as smartphones, tablet devices, etc., are available for use in a secure mobile environment.

In February 2015, Cisco Japan won the Excellence Award at the Japan Productivity Center Empowerment Awards. There are four points which were recognized: 1) Set I&C as business imperative, 2) Establish I&C team structure to enhance awareness and promote behavior changes, 3) Promote "Cross Cultural Connection", "Connected Women" and "Flexible Work Practice" and 4) Drive flexible work practices with Cisco technologies.

女性リーダー育成プログラム
Project Quantum

　シスコのインクルージョン＆コラボレーション推進の大きな柱である女性活躍推進の一環として日本におけるシスコで生まれたのが、管理職候補育成プログラム「Project Quantum」です。このプログラムは2014年1月から始まりました。

　女性の活躍は世界的課題ですが、なかでも日本は、2015年のダボス会議で出たジェンダーギャップ（男女格差）指数が101位ということでも明らかなように、ジェンダーダイバーシティ（性多様性）は低いレベルにあります。それは、ダイバーシティを早くから推進してきたシスコの中でさえ課題です。シスコ日本法人には女性社員が20％在籍していますが、女性のピープルマネージャー（部下を持つ管理職）は非常に少ないことにも表れています。マネージャーの眼からみると優秀な女性が大勢いるのに、なぜかリーダーのポジションについていないと言われてきました。そこには控え目で男性を立てるのが賢い女性とされてきた日本社会の旧習が影響を残しているとも考えられます。「Project Quantum」は、リーダーシップの潜在力を持つ女性社員たちがプログラムによって得た学びを礎に成長を続け、「Quantum＝飛躍」してほしい、広く活躍してほしいという願いを込めた命名でした。

　Project Quantumが育成を目指すリーダーは、ピープルマネージャーだけではなく、1つのプロジェクトのリーダーや何らかのイニシアティブを取るようなリーダーシップを発揮する人材

46

です。

　人事・教育の部署にジェンダーダイバーシティの担当者も加わり、1年間の継続的なプログラムが計画され、マネージャーから推薦された参加メンバーが集まりました。

　セールス部門から、マーケティング部門から、プログラム部門から、テクニカル部門から……専門性も社歴もさまざまで、それまでほとんど面識もなかったメンバーが最初に取り組むのは「270度アセスメント」です。270度とは自分自身、上司、同僚であり、その評価を見つめます。将来部下ができればそれは360度になります。

　評価によって自分自身のリーダーとしてのありかたや強み、これから注力して伸ばすべき点を知り、その後のキャリアについての話し合いに活用します。キャリアについての話し合いは、上司と定期的に行って中長期の自分の成長計画を立てます。

　シスコには3E（Education, Experience, Exposure）という社員育成の考え方があり、Project Quantumもそれに則ったカリキュラムで進められます。

▎ Education（学習する）

　シスコがグローバルで展開する管理職候補育成トレーニング「JUMP」を、講師を招いてスクール形式のトレーニングで行います。2日間で、自分のリーダーとしてのありかたを認識し、それに基づいてキャリアプラン、成長計画の立て方、助言者や賛同者の見つけ方、自分のイメージの確立（ブランディング）について学びます。

47

Experience（経験を通して学ぶ）

現在の業務範囲以外の経験をすることでスキルを身につけるストレッチ アサインメント、メンバー同士でプログラムで得た経験や意見を共有する会議、先輩や指導者からの助言や指導、有識者によるキャリアについての話、外部ダイバーシティについての専門家会議への参加などさまざまな経験を積みます。

話し合うことで学び、新たな気づきを得たり、影響を与え合うことや、4半期に1回行われる教育担当者との2時間近い個人面談は、新たな洞察や自身の能力の発見等、多くの収穫を得る課程です。

Exposure（人を通して学ぶ）

所属部門以外の役員や本部長クラスの役員に随行するシャドーイング プログラムを行います。他部門への理解を深め、時には外部との打ち合わせにも同席し、役員の考え方や行動を学びます。リーダーの意思決定のプロセスを身近に目のあたりにするシャドーイングは、Project Quantumにおける最高の体験です。

ITは変化の速い業界です。ロール（role）が替わることも度々なので、適応力の高い人が求められます。専門的な能力もマネージメント能力もともに必要です。Project Quantumの直近の目標は女性のピープルマネージャーを増やすことですが、さらに上のグレードを目指すことは周囲からも期待されることです。

シスコ日本法人の女性社員はしばしば「もっと自信を持て」と

指摘されます。抜擢を打診されると「そんな大役はとても自信が
ありません」としり込みしてしまう人が多いのです。シスコほど
フレックスが徹底していて、どこでも仕事ができるインフラが
整備された企業は多くありません。そんな環境にありながら不
足していたのは、リーダーになる資質ではなく、自らの可能性
を信じる強い気持ちだったのです。マインドの改革、そこにI＆
Cの本当の意味があります。

　Project Quantumは、参加者たちが主導した点が大きな特色
です。トレーニングに喜びを感じることが成長につながりまし
た。

　第一期の最後に行った全員参加の討論では「この1年間で学ん
だことを後輩に伝える」というテーマでした。そこに出たたくさ
んのメッセージをまとめたのが本書です。それは参加者自身の
発想によるものです。

　シスコ社内向けに制作された初版は、アメリカ、ヨーロッパ、
アジアのシスコ各社から購入希望が殺到。対外的にも2014年
11月に香港で行われた60企業のダイバーシティのカンファレ
ンスで紹介されました。

　そして今ここに、一般の書籍として販売され、広く日本の女
性たちの役に立つことになったのです。

49●

Project Quantumプログラム

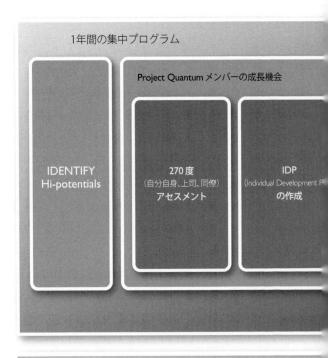

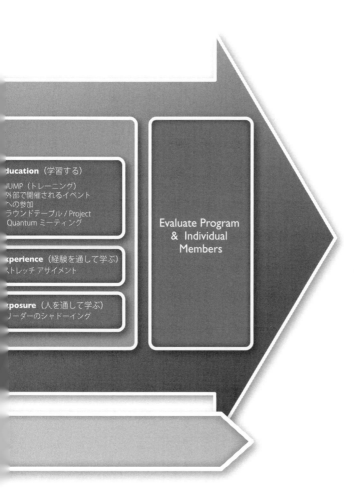

Project Quantum:
Fostering female leaders

Cisco initiated Project Quantum, a program fostering female leaders, to enhance women's corporate advancement, a key component of the company's inclusion and collaboration efforts. The program was launched in January 2014.

As global societies struggle with the issue of female advancement, Japan's own challenge with gender diversity was highlighted at the 2015 World Economic Forum in Davos, where the country received a Global Gender Gap ranking of 101 among the world's nations. Diversity is an issue even within Cisco, which addressed the problem early on. Some 20% of Cisco Japan's work force is female, but "people managers" (those with subordinates) remain extremely few in number. We have come to understand that, although managers identify many outstanding females, they somehow do not assign them to leadership positions. This may be due to residual influences from old Japan, where clever women remained in the background while urging the men forward.

Project Quantum was named in hopes that female participants with management potential would build on what they had learned and make a quantum leap into active leadership.

Leaders fostered by Project Quantum are not only people managers, but also those who can seize the reins of initiative and demonstrate leadership in a given project.

Those in charge of gender diversity in our human resources and educations sections helped plan the year-long program for participants who would be recommended by managers.

Participants, scarcely acquainted with each other in most cases, originated from marketing, programming, technical, and other departments, and represented varying corporate backgrounds and areas of expertise. Their first task was to perform a 270-degree assessment, or evaluation of oneself, one's superiors, and one's peers. Assessment of one's subordinates at some future point would complete the 360-degree circle.

Evaluating oneself helps strengthen personal leadership, indicates areas needing focus for growth, and affords practical application in subsequent discussions about one's career, which should occur regularly with one's superior and involve creation of mid-range career plans.

Cisco believes in incorporating the 3Es (Education, Experience, Exposure) into employee training, and Project Quantum follows suit in its curriculum.

Education

Project Quantum incorporates lecturers for classroom training in much the same way that Cisco has expanded its own leadership training program known as JUMP. Over a two-day period, participants first gain awareness of the type of leader they aspire to be, using that as a springboard to establish a career plan. They learn how to formulate a growth strategy, find a mentor and advocates, and zero in on a self-image (branding).

Experience

Project Quantum participants enjoy a wide range of experiences, beginning with a "stretch assignment," in which individuals expand a non-vocational task which will afford them new skills. Participants also discuss experiences and opinions they have encountered in the program during meetings, enjoy advice and guidance from superiors and leaders, hear experts speak on careers, and participate in external professional conferences on diversity.

The course bears many fruits for participants, offering new insights and discoveries about their abilities as they learn through discussion, new awareness, chances to impact each other, and a nearly two-hour private interview with the head of training every quarter.

Exposure

Project Quantum incorporates a shadowing program providing exposure to executives from other departments as well as to top management, allowing deeper understanding of those in such positions. Participants also sit in on meetings between internal and external executives, absorbing how managers conduct themselves. Shadowing, which sees leaders' decision-making process unfold before participants' very eyes, represents the ultimate Project Quantum experience.

Things change rapidly in the IT industry, as do the roles played by those involved. The field is best suited to highly adaptable individuals. Both professional expertise and management skills are a must. Project Quantum's immediate goal is to increase the participation of women in people management positions, but there is also expectation of seeing them ultimately aim for even higher-level positions as well.

Female employees at Cisco Japan are repeatedly advised to have greater self-confidence. When approached about major promotions, many balk and profess a lack of confidence about leaping into such an important position. Cisco is unusual among corporations for its flex-time infrastructure allowing women to work with ease in any location. What has been missing in this work environment is not leadership characteristics, but rather self-confidence and a strong belief in oneself. The real meaning of inclusion and collaboration lies in a transformation of the mind.

One of the most striking characteristics of Project Quantum is the initiative demonstrated by participants. Taking delight in the training process is a sure sign of growth.

The inaugural program concluded with a discussion (attended by all participants) on sharing wisdom gained during the year-long program with junior colleagues. This book is a compilation of those many lessons, all of which reflect participants' own thoughts.

There has been a rush of requests from Cisco group companies in the US, Europe, and Asia for the first edition of this book, which targets in-house readers. The work has also enjoyed external exposure — namely, to 60 companies participating in a diversity conference in Hong Kong in November 2014.

And now, the book enters the general market for sale, demonstrating that it continues to be of great service to Japanese women.

Project Quantum メンバーからのメッセージ
Messages from Project Quantum Members

第1章
「チャレンジ」

Chapter 1
Challenge

チャレンジ/Challenge

光が見えたとき、
変化は
孤独ではなくなる

Leading can be lonely. But there is always light at the end of tunnel

チャレンジ /Challenge

　率先する、初めの一歩を踏み出す、リーダーシップを発揮する……これらはすべて勇気がいる行動でしょう。新しいことを始めようとするときはいつでも、自分ひとりで世界に立ち向かっていくような感覚に陥ってしまうものです。

　でも大丈夫。ビジョンや理想を掲げて未来を思い描き、リーダーシップをとって旅路を進みましょう。やがて何かが変わったら、周囲はあなたの努力に気づき始めるはずです。

　そのとき、あなたはもうひとりではありません。思いは必ずみんなに伝わります。素晴らしい変化はいつだって初めの一歩を踏み出す勇気から生まれるのです。

　Acting first. Making the first move. Taking the lead. All these are actions that require courage. When you start something new… at first it is only you and the world… many times you are alone.

　But that is OK. A leader starts with a first courageous step in search of a higher vision, a higher ideal, a better tomorrow. Continue your journey of leadership and then something happens: you realize that people start noticing your efforts.

　You realize you are no longer alone. Leadership is contagious… All great things start with the first step.

チャレンジ /Challenge

変化を楽しむ

●

Enjoy change

チャレンジ /Challenge

　あなたにとって変化とは何ですか？　それは何かの始まりであり、ときにはチャンスともなります。つまり、進化や変革をもたらす人生のエッセンスです。

　大切なのは、人生で避けて通ることのできない変化を、友のような存在として受け容れること。変化は、新たな物事を学ぶチャンスをくれる、かけがえのない友人です。

　新たな環境を迷わず迎え入れて、前向きに活躍していきましょう。どうか変化を楽しんで！

　　What is change? Change is an opening. Change is an opportunity. Change is the essence of life. Change drives evolution and transformation.

　　It is important to see change as a friend. Change does not go away. Embrace change and make change your friend. Change is an opportunity to learn new things.

　　Learn to adapt, learn to lead in a new environment. Have fun!

チャレンジ /Challenge

楽しむ方法を
見つける

●

Make it fun

チャレンジ /Challenge

　日々の仕事やチャレンジ、新たなプロジェクト、課題、目標……限られた時間しかない中でやるべきことが山積みになっていると、圧倒されて身動きが取れないと感じるかもしれません。
　そんなときこそ、みんなで力を合わせて何かを成し遂げた際の達成感を思い出してみましょう。想像をめぐらせ、何をするにも楽しさや喜びを感じられる方法を見つけてください。

　Work, challenges, new project, new tasks, new targets…. It is easy to get overwhelmed, bogged down. So much to do, so little time.
　We need to remember the fun, the excitement, the joy that comes with the effort on working on ourselves. Be creative: Find ways to bring fun and joy into everything you do!

チャレンジ /Challenge

ステップ アップ することは 楽しい!

●

Stepping up is fun!

チャレンジ /Challenge

　努力することをつらいと感じる人もいますが、本当にそうでしょうか。難しい目標を達成するまでの過程、そして達成したときの満足感は何物にも代えがたいものです。

　小さな子どもは、常に新しいことに挑戦しようとする、あくなき探究心に満ちています。達成までの過程をも楽しんでいるから、学ぶ意欲がどんどん湧き出てくるのです。

　リーダーシップを発揮するのも同じことがいえます。学ぶ楽しさを味わいながら、新しい自分へとステップ アップしましょう。何事にも笑顔でぶつかっていって！

　　Whoever said that hard work is hard was utterly wrong. Accomplishing something challenging is one of the most satisfying things you can do. Along the way you also can have a lot of fun.

　　Look at small children. They are the most avid leaners, the most tireless minds that are constantly trying new things. Look at all the fun they have a long the way! They always come back for more.

　　Your leadership work is the same. Step up to a new you. Fun is yours for the taking. Smile and charge ahead!

チャレンジ /Challenge

機会を受け入れる

●

Learn to welcome opportunities

チャレンジ /Challenge

　リーダーとなるチャンスがやって来たら、あなたはどうしますか？そのチャンスを受け入れますか？　それとも戸惑って気づかなかったふりをしますか？
　恐れやためらいを脱ぎ捨て立ち上がりましょう。成長をサポートしてくれる新たなチャンスを喜んで迎え入れ、最大限に活かしてください。

　The chance to lead knocks on your door. Where are you? Will you dare open the door and welcome the challenge? Or will you shy away and pretend you did not hear it?

　Stand up, take the challenge. Overcome your fears and hesitations. New opportunities come to you to help you grow and develop. Make the most of it. Welcome them with a smiling face.

チャレンジ /Challenge

もう一歩先へ

●

Take
one more step

チャレンジ /Challenge

　逆境に直面すると、成功への道を阻むいくつもの障害が目の前に立ちはだかっているように感じるかもしれません。そういうときこそ真の力が問われるものです。

　勇気を奮い起して、努力を惜しまず進んでいきましょう。自分の限界は自分で超えていくものです。

　決意の力はあなたが想像している以上にパワフルです。意志あるところに道は必ず開けるから、一歩一歩前進していきましょう。

　When the going gets tough, the tough get going. Obstacles can appear to block your way to success. Persevere and do not give in.

　Gather the strength and go one step further. You impose on you your own limitations. You have the power to expand your mind and go the extra mile.

　Never underestimate the power of your determination. Where there is a will, there is a way. Take that extra step.

チャレンジ /Challenge

スピーク アップ!

●

Speak up !

チャレンジ /Challenge

　恐れや気恥ずかしさ、自信のなさが邪魔をして、発言を躊躇したりあきらめてしまったりすることがあるでしょう。

　どんな理由にせよ、声を上げなければ誰の耳にも届きません。考えを言葉にしなければ、有意義な会話は生まれず、誰からも意見を得ることはできず、革新的なアイデアが生まれることもないのです。

　自分の考えを話そうとすれば、相手はあなたを見つめ、耳を傾け、発言を理解しようと努めてくれます。まずは小さな発言から始めて、少しずつ上手に伝えられるようにしていきましょう。何かを発言することは、自分の考えを知ってもらい、周囲に自分を理解してもらうチャンスと捉えてください。

　For a variety of reasons, you may find that sometimes you hold yourself back, you hesitate, you fail to speak up when you should. It could be fear, it could be shyness, it could be lack of confidence.

　Whatever the reason, remember that if you do not speak up, you will not be heard. If you do not voice your thoughts, the discussion will be less richer, less diverse, less innovative. Let your point of view be known, do not fear anything.

　People will look at you and listen to what you bring to the table. Start with small trials and work your way up from there. When you speak up, you are giving yourself a chance to be heard and others a chance to understand you.

チャレンジ/Challenge

何かを学ぶために
ここにいる

●

You are here to
learn something

チャレンジ /Challenge

　日々生まれる疑問は、何かを学べる有効なツールです。なぜ自分はここにいるのか、何にチャレンジするべきか、経験から何が得られるのか、自分自身に問いかけてみましょう。自分について、会社について、同僚について、自分の環境や知識について……答えが何であれ、そこには必ず学びがあるものです。
　そう考えれば、学ぶということは生きる道であり生き方そのものであり、決して終わりはないと気づくはず。さあ、今日はいったい何が学べるでしょう？

　Questions are useful tools. Questions have answers in themselves. What are you here for? What is the learning opportunity? What is the challenge? What is the lesson from a particular experience? Whatever the answer, you are here, today, to learn something. To learn something about yourself, about your company, about your peers, about your environment, about your culture, about your world, etc.

　When you think like this, you realize that learning is an endless journey. A path and a way of living. Today you are here to learn. What will you learn today?

チャレンジ /Challenge

目標は高く持つこと

●

Set your goals high

チャレンジ /Challenge

　目標を立てるときは少し欲張ってみましょう。可能性は果てしなく、どこに限界があるかなど誰にもわかりません。チャレンジングな目標をじっくりと立てたときはいつだって、自分の想像以上の成果が得られるものです。

　一流の芸術家やアスリート、パフォーマーなどはとても高い目標を設定します。自分の限界を超え、日々の進歩を実感しながら挑戦し続けているのです。

　さらなる高みを目指して努力すれば、明日は今日より成長した自分にきっと出会えるはずです。

　Be aggressive when setting goals to yourself. Who knows the extent of your boundless potential? Nobody has the answer to that question. You can stretch and achieve more than you can possibly imagine, if only you take the time to set goals that are inspiring and challenging.

　Great artists, great athletes, great performers set lofty goals for themselves. Nature works through stretching, through gently evolving and moving to a better tomorrow.

　Aim high. Tomorrow you will stand from a higher ground than today.

チャレンジ/Challenge

5年プランを立ててみる

●

Build a five-year plan

チャレンジ /Challenge

　5年のキャリアプランを立ててみる方法は、あなたにぴったりかもしれません。どのようなスキルを身につけ、どのような役職につき、どのようなプロジェクトに挑戦したいですか。今の自分が持つ経験と違いがあるかどうかを見極めてみましょう。

　5年プランは完璧でなくても大丈夫。キャリアの方向性を示す旅程表のようなものだから、途中で修正してもいいのです。

　夢を大きく持ってワクワクしながら5年プランを立ててみましょう。あとは実行に移すのみです。

　This is a tool that you might like to consider using: Try building a 5 year career plan. What skills you would like to acquire? What roles would you like to experience? What projects you would like to be involved in? What experience gaps do you currently have? How will you cover for them?

　The 5 year plan does not have to be perfect. It can be a working document, like a travel chart of the direction you would like to take your career into.

　Make a 5 year plan. Have fun with it. Dream big. Take action.

チャレンジ/Challenge

長期的な
ライフ プランを
持つ

Have a long
term plan

ライフ プランを持つことは、長期的な視野で物事を見つめ、優先したいことを考える絶好の機会となります。キャリアと家庭のバランスをどのように取るか、ライフ ステージごとに何に専念するか。限られた時間を有効に使うためには、優先すべきことを見つめ直し、時間の管理をすることが大切です。

どんなキャリア パスをたどり、どんな経験を積めそうか、自分が立てたライフ プランと向き合ってみましょう。自分の進むべき道を探るためのヒントが必ず見つかるはずです。

Having a life plan is a good idea. It can give you perspective and make you think about the priorities you would like to embrace. Time is limited, you need to be a good steward of your time. How will you use it? What will you prioritize? How will you balance your career with family life? There are different stages in life that will require different levels of dedication and time management.

Read about career paths and life experiences. It will help you find what is the journey you would like to have with your own life.

チャレンジ /Challenge

ひとつ上の
視点を持つ

●

Elevate
your point of
view

チャレンジ /Challenge

　人は自分が立っている場所から物事を見ます。視点は自分を取り巻く世界を分析するために使うレンズのようなもの。セールス部門に所属していれば営業担当者の視点で、財務であればコントローラーの視点で、エンジニアであれば技術的な視点で、管理職ならば自分の部署の管理者としての視点で物事を見て、問題を分析します。

　一度、自分の視点を引き上げてみてください。ためしに自分の上司やそのまた上司の視点で物事を見てみると、より高度で広い視野を持って問題を捉えられるはずです。

　自分が存在している箱の中から抜け出して、全体を広く見渡せることの自由と素晴らしさを味わってみてください。

　We look at issues from where we stand. Our point of view becomes the lenses we use to see and assess our universe. If you are in Sales, you see things as a sales person. If you are in Finance, you see issues like a controller. If you are in Engineering, you see problems from a technical perspective. If you are a manager, you view the world as a manager of your department.

　Next time, try this: Elevate your point of view. Look at the issue from the point of view of your manager, of your manager's manager. Look at problems thinking a bit higher, a bit broader.

　Come out of the box you find yourself in. Taste the freedom and joy that comes from a higher vantage point.

チャレンジ /Challenge

リスクを恐れない

●

Take risks

チャレンジ /Challenge

　勇気を出して、危ない橋を渡ることやリスクも恐れない、アクティブ志向になりましょう。向こう見ずになるという意味ではありません。恐れを捨てて勇気を奮い立たせ、自分が達成できる最大限の可能性を目指すということです。

　果敢に行動できる人には運がめぐってくるもの。リスクを負う勇気を持ちましょう。

　　Be bold. Take risks. Be action-orientated. Live dangerously. This is not an invitation to be reckless. It is a calling to be brave and courageous. To leave behind your fears and aspire for the very best you can achieve.

　　Fortune favors the bold. Take risks.

チャレンジ/Challenge

後戻りしてもよい

●

You can always go back

チャレンジ /Challenge

　その道が自分にとって正しいかどうか、それが自分に合っているかどうかは、挑戦や経験をしないことにはわかりません。

　遊び心を忘れず新しいことに挑んでみましょう。自分の力を発揮できる分野がより明確になるかもしれません。途中で後戻りをしたり、方向性を変えたり、立ち止まったりしてもいいのです。修正と失敗は同じことではありません。

　好奇心を持って探究し、自分に最適な道を見つけてください。

　　Sometimes you do not know if a path is for you until you try it. Sometimes you do not know if you will enjoy doing something until you experience it.

　　Be playful and experiment with new things, you may learn new things and gain greater clarity on where your strengths truly lie. Remember it is OK to go back. It is OK to course-correct and adjust. Do not confuse correction with failure. They are 2 different things.

　　Be curious and inquisitive. Find the right path for you.

チャレンジ /Challenge

常に代替案を

●

Have a plan B

　常に目標を思い描きながら行動し、自分がしたいこと、すべきことを理解していることでしょう。けれども変化し続ける世界において、代替案を立てておくのは大切なことです。

　失敗を想定したりあきらめたりするという意味ではありません。代替案を立てることで自由になり、心の余裕が生まれ、何が起ころうとも取るべき行動が明確になるということです。

　代替案を立てる習慣を身につければ、クリエイティブかつ革新的になれます。ときには元のプランを早く成功させることにもつながるでしょう。

　We always move with a goal in mind. We know what we want and what we need to do. But in this ever-changing dynamic world, it is important to have a back-up plan.

　Have a Plan B, not because you plan to fail or give up, but because a Plan B will give you the freedom and extra peace of mind to know that you will know what to do regardless of what happens.

　Getting into the habit of having a Plan B allows you to be more creative and innovative. Sometimes, while thinking of a Plan B, you may come across a great idea to make your Plan A succeed even faster. It pays to be thoughtful.

Project Quantum メンバーからのメッセージ
Messages from Project Quantum Members

第2章
「コミュニケーション」
「ネットワーキング」

Chapter 2
Communication
Networking

コミュニケーション /Communication

話せば
新しい道が
見つかる

●

Talking leads to solutions and understanding

コミュニケーション /Communication

　誰かと意見が対立したとき、何を優先すべきか迷つたとき、問題に直面したとき……そんなときこそ落ち着いて冷静な視点で物事を見つめ、話し合いやディスカッションを積極的に進めることが大切です。話し合うことを恐れず、きちんと正面から向き合って解決策を導き出しましょう。

　We find conflict. We find competing priorities. We hit a roadblock. That is the time to keep your cool, keep your poise and lead the way by leading the dialogue, leading the discussion. Do not be afraid of talking things out. Do not hide. Talk it out, find a solution.

コミュニケーション / Communication

自分の言葉に
置き換えて伝える

Internalize your learning. Share them with all

コミュニケーション /Communication

　本や資料を読む、実践する、試行錯誤する、観察する……学ぶにはさまざまな方法があります。

　得たばかりの知識やスキルの力はもろく、また新たな見解を自分の言葉に置き換えて伝えるのは簡単なことではありません。

　書くことでアウトプットしたり、親しい友人や同僚と議論や共有を重ねたりすることで知識やスキルは成熟し、やがて自分のものとして定着していきます。そのときこそ本当にステップ アップした自分に気づくはずです。

　　How do you learn? By reading? By doing? By trying things out? By observation? There are many ways of approaching the learning process.

　　New knowledge can be fragile. New skills and insights can be hard to put into words.

　　Here is where you need to push forward. Find a way to put your new knowledge into words, find a way to internalize your learning. Share it with others. Discuss it, write about it, share it with a close friend or a colleague. Then you will see that the learning matures, the new skill gains strength and you have developed a step higher than yesterday.

コミュニケーション /Communication

相手の立場を考えた コミュニケーション を取る

●

Be a skillful communicator. Put yourself in others' shoes

コミュニケーション /Communication

　もしあなたがコミュニケーション スキルの高い人なら、言葉、意味、理解が双方向で交わされることこそがコミュニケーションであるとわかるでしょう。真のコミュニケーション スキルとは、相手の立場になって考え、相手を理解し、そのうえで自分の意見を提示する能力のことです。
　人は皆異なる人間です。どのように表現すれば自分の意見を理解してもらえるか、よく考える必要があります。コミュニケーションは芸術。鑑賞者が何を求めているかを汲み取り、素敵な「芸術作品」をつくりあげる方法を学びましょう。

　Are you a skillful communicator? If yes, you know that communication is a flow. A flow of words, a flow of meaning and a flow of understanding. And the flow works both ways. Communication is a skill that is ever aware, ever present, ever conscious of the other party.
　All people are different and so you need to be aware of how you can better communicate and express your views. Communication is an art. Learn this art by paying close attention to the needs of your audience.

コミュニケーション /Communication

Noという勇気

●

Have the courage to say NO

コミュニケーション /Communication

　上司やプロジェクト マネージャー、パートナー、友人などは相手に何かをお願いするとき、引き受けてくれることを期待しているでしょう。引き受けられる場合もあれば、他に優先すべきことがあるなど事情によって断らざるを得ない場合もあります。

　No と言うべき場面で Yes と言ってしまったことが、これまでに何度あるでしょうか。なぜ No と言えなかったのか、なぜ思いとどまってしまったのかを考えてみましょう。社会的なプレッシャーや義務を感じたのかもしれないし内気な性格が原因かもしれない、あるいは断った場合の相手の反応を恐れたのかもしれません。どんな理由であれ、ときには意思表示をすることも大切だと覚えておいてください。Yes か No か、どちらの答えを選ぶにしても勇気を持って返事をしましょう。

　It could be your boss, your partner, your friend or a project manager... They have an ask from you. They want you to comply, they want you to agree. There are times when YES is indeed the answer to give. But there are times when you need to prioritize and for one reason or another you need to push back, you need to say NO.

　How many times have you said YES when you needed to say NO? What stopped you? What held you back? Social pressures, sense of duty, perhaps a bit of shyness? Fear of the reaction if you said no? Whatever it was, please know there are times when you need to speak your mind and bring your point across. Courage is present in YES and in NO… whatever your choice, allow courage to guide your answer.

コミュニケーション /Communication

英語での
コミュニケーションが
世界を広げる

English communication expands your world

コミュニケーション/Communication

　日本語を話さない人々との会話や、英語で書かれた資料の読み込みなど、英語を視野を広げるためのツールとして活用しましょう。英語でのコミュニケーションは、あなたにとっても相手にとっても学びがあるものです。英語を使うことで自分の視野だけでなく他の人の視野をも広げることができるのです。

　English is a tool. Use it to expand your horizons. Reach out to people and resources that are not available in Japanese. This reaching out is a two-way street. You learn and the other party learns from you too. English not only helps you expand your horizons but you expand someone else's too.

コミュニケーション /Communication

クリアな
メッセージング

●

Nothing beats
clarity

コミュニケーション /Communication

　メッセージが半分しか伝わっていないとしたら、それは本当に伝えたいことがたくさんの言葉の中に埋もれてしまっているのかもしれません。考えを明確にすればはっきりとした表現が生まれるし、はっきりとした表現を用いれば伝えたいことの意味もわかりやすくなります。そして、意味がわかりやすくなればより深い理解を得られるのです。

　正しい見識があれば、あなたのメッセージはみんなに伝わります。ミーティングに入る前や議論を行う前などに、自分の考えは明確か、意味をしっかりと伝えることができるか、そして十分に理解してもらえるかどうかを確認しましょう。

　　A message half-delivered is a message lost in a sea of words. Clarity of thought leads to clarity of words. Clarity of words leads to clarity of meaning. Clarity of meaning leads to clarity of understanding.

　　And when you have the right understanding, your message is a clear as it needs to be. Before going into your meeting, into your review or whatever it may be, lead with clarity of thought and see that your meaning finds fulfillment and flowers in understanding.

コミュニケーション /Communication

アイ コンタクト

●

Keep eye contact

コミュニケーション /Communication

　目は心の窓。思いを伝えるときはしっかりと相手の目を見るようにしましょう。自分の考えを主張したり力強いプレゼンテーションを行ったりするときは、しっかりとアイ コンタクトを取ることが大切です。自信は目の輝きに表れます。そして明確な意思は声のトーンやしっかりとしたアイ コンタクトで示すことができるのです。

　Some people say that the eyes are windows to the soul. We use our eyes to see and communicate. Assert yourself and add strength to your presentations with unequivocal eye contact. Your confidence will shine through your eyes. Your engagement will show in the tone of your voice and the power of your eye contact.

コミュニケーション /Communication

間を活用する

●

Use pauses

コミュニケーション /Communication

　何かを話すときやプレゼンテーションを行うとき、緊張から駆け足で進めてしまいがちです。焦らず落ち着いてゆっくりと話し、ときどき間を挟むようにしましょう。

　自信を持って安心して話せるように、話の構成をきちんと準備しておいたり、今話題となっている事柄について把握したりしておくことも大切です。伝えるべきことや行うべきことはわかっているはずなので、あとは間を上手に用いることを意識しましょう。それによって、伝えたいことを強調するだけでなく、聞いている人々から送られるサインを察知し、場の一体感をつくり出すこともできるのです。

　Do not rush when you talk, when you present. Even if nervous, avoid the tendency to rush through something. Take your time. PAUSE.

　Compose yourself and go back to that place of comfort and confidence, where you are the master of your subject. You know what you need to say and convey. You know what you can do. Use pauses skillfully, not only to accentuate your meaning but to also connect with the audience and ensure you are not missing any important cues from your listeners.

ネットワーキング / **Networking**

どんなところにも
ネットワークをつくる
チャンスがある

●

You can expand
your network
anywhere

ネットワーキング / Networking

　ネットワークはいつでもどこにいても広がる可能性があるものです。主体的な姿勢で、長期的で意義ある人間関係を築くチャンスへの感度を高めましょう。自分とは異なる人々から多くのことを学べるよう、ネットワークを広げていってください。

　結びつきがより重要となる今の時代、意義ある関係を築くことはビジネスだけでなく個人としても飛躍的な成長に結びつきます。そのチャンスを逃すことなくつかみ取りましょう。

　Extending your network can happen literally at any time. No matter the place or the time. The ownership and initiative rests in you. Be open to opportunities to create lasting meaningful relationships. Expand your reach. Seek out to learn from people from other walks of life.

　In this age of interconnectedness, building meaningful relationships can lead to exponential growth, not only in business but personal growth too. Seize the day!

ネットワーキング / Networking

知る、話す、そして刺激し合える仲間を持つ

●

Befriend stimulating people eager to learn and do more

ネットワーキング / Networking

　ネットワークを広げることは学びや継続的な成長に欠かせません。物事の基準となるもの、刺激を与えてくれるものを社外にも求めてみましょう。ロール モデルとなる人を見つけたり、多様な見方や異なる感覚、新たなアイデアや人々に触れたりするのは素晴らしいことです。成長を促すだけでなく、チャンスを引き寄せる新たな活路を生み出してくれるでしょう。

　Expanding your network of people is critical to learning and continuous progression. You need an external benchmark, you need the stimulation, you need to have roles models, diverse views, different perceptions, expose yourself to new ideas and people. You not only accelerate your own development but create new pathways for opportunities to gravitate to you.

ネットワーキング / **Networking**

社内ネットワーキングは大切

●

Your internal network has power

ネットワーキング / Networking

　企業で働くということは、社内だけでも何千人もの人と知り合うチャンスに恵まれているということ。そしてすべての人とのコミュニケーションが学びの機会となり得るのです。

　社内のネットワークは、自分の中のツール ボックスに新たな機能を加えてくれます。多くの気づきを与えてくれ、あなたをより向上させてくれるでしょう。

　今自分が置かれている環境を過小評価しないでください。身近にある物事を最高な形で活用できるチャンスをあなたは持っているのです。

　With thousands of employees, you have the opportunity of thousands of encounters within your own company. Each encounter can bring with it the opportunities for new learnings.

　Building your internal network can help you bring new capabilities to your toolbox. It can expand your awareness and inspire you to reach new heights.

　Never underestimate your environment. Sometimes the best things are right next to you, waiting for you to harness them.

ネットワーキング / Networking

支援してくれる人は身近にいる

●

There is always someone ready to support you

　手を差し伸べてくれたり成長をサポートしてくれたりする存在は、誰にとっても欠かせないものです。周囲の人々はあなたが考える以上に心を配ってくれているもの。視野を広げて周りを見回し、スポンサーを見つけましょう。

　ミーティングへ招待したりメールで連絡したりなど、ときには自ら行動を起こす勇気も必要です。自発的に声をかけることで、手を貸してくれる人がきっと見つかるはずです。

　スポンサーたちはいつでもあなたのそばにいます。必要なときに助けを受け入れられるよう準備し、そして学ぶ姿勢を整えておきましょう。

　　We all need sponsors. Someone who will help us and advocate for our growth and development. People care more than we think they do. Look around, expand your views and find your sponsor.

　　Sometimes all it takes is a bit of courage. Sometimes all it takes is a call. A meeting invite, an e-mail…and there you have it… a helping hand ready to assist.

　　Looks around. Ask. Be ready to receive the help you need. Be open to learn.

Project Quantum メンバーからのメッセージ
Messages from Project Quantum Members

第3章
「影響力」
「ダイバーシティ」

Chapter 3
Influence
Diversity

影響力 / Influence

与えるインパクトを
常に考える

●

Always think
about IMPACT

影響力 / Influence

　人は物事に自分なりの優先順位をつけ、それに基づいて行動する生き物です。行動は目標やゴールに左右されがちですが、何かをする前に一度こう自問してみてください。
　この行動はどんなインパクトを与えられるだろう？この行動によって私が本当に達成しようとしていることは何だろう？
　周りに与えるインパクトを優先して考え、意義のある行動を取るよう心がけましょう。そのためには、目的も持たずただ何かをするのではなく、どんなインパクトを与えられるかをはっきりと意識することです。
　可能性は無限です。方向性を決め、さらなる向上を目指して進んでいってください。

　　We are driven by our priorities. Ultimately, our aims and goals define where we go. Before taking a course of action, ask yourself:
　　What is the IMPACT of this action? What am I really trying achieve?
　　Prioritize IMPACT. Do something meaningful. Bring IMPACT to the front. Say NO to doing things for the sake of doing them.
　　You set the tone, the target is wide open. Aim for the highest peak.

影響力 / Influence

多くの人たちと
交流を持つ

Engage others

影響力 / Influence

　私たちは皆、常に誰かとつながっているということを忘れがちです。交流を持つことは人々をつなぐ「接着剤」となるばかりでなく、身の回りの環境に影響を与えたり、自分や相手に変化をもたらしたりもします。上司や同僚、他部署の人、あるいは異業種のプロフェッショナルなど、たくさんの人々と交流をはかってください。

　さあ、今こそ自分という枠を壊しましょう。豊かな発想ができるよう、さまざまな人たちと積極的に関わりを持つようにしてください。

　Many times we tend to forget we are all connected. Our interactions are the glue that join us together, and ALSO the medium through which we exert influence on our environment. Changing yourself and changing others begins and ends with engagement. Engage your boss, engage your peers, engage your colleagues from other departments, engage professionals from other industries.

　Come out of your box. This is the real meaning of thinking "outside-the-box". ENGAGE.

影響力 / Influence

自分の行動の結果を
よく考える

●

Take the time
to think things

影響力 / Influence

　情報時代にいる私たちは、限りないデータや情報によって注意力や判断力を鈍らせ、反射的に行動を起こすというわなに落ちています。あふれ返るほどの情報にあやつられ、自分自身で考えるということを怠ってしまっているのです。

　自分の貴重な能力やエネルギーを本来どこでどのように使うべきか、よく考えてみましょう。そして新たな未来をきちんと見据えられるよう先見の明を養うことが大切です。

　In this information age you are constantly flooded with endless data, endless information, endless things bombarding our attention. In fact, your actions in many cases tend to be almost automatic. Avoid that trap. Do not become over-informed yet under-reflected.

　Take the time to think things through, take the time to sit down and ponder "where" and "how" you should be spending your precious energy. Aim to become a visionary. Someone with vision to a new future.

影響力 / Influence

社内外に
ロール モデルを持つ

●

Have a role model

影響力 / Influence

　小さいころは親がロール モデルだったことでしょう。親の話すこと、歩く姿、仕草などをじっと見つめ、同じことを少しずつ学びましたよね。成長して大人になり、新たなロール モデルを見つけることをいつしか忘れてしまったのではないでしょうか。

　学ぶことは人生そのもの。いくつになっても学ぶことはあります。自分の可能性を現実的な視点で見つめられたり、さまざまなことを効果的に学べたりできる、それがロール モデルです。

　興味や趣味の範囲を広げ、社内外問わずたくさんのロール モデルを見つけましょう。世界は、類まれな功績を収めた意欲的な人たちであふれているのです。

　When we are little, our parents are our role models. We look at them and see them speak, walk and move. Little by little we learn to do the same as them. We grow up and become adults and somehow along the way we forget to deliberately make new roles models.

　Learning never stops. It is part of life. Learning is life. A role model helps expedite learning, it provides a real-life picture of what is possible. Have plenty of role models both within and outside the company.

　Bring diversity to your favor. Have diverse role models. The world is full of examples of great bravery and exceptional achievement.

影響力 / Influence

社内外に
メンターを持つ

Have a mentor

　メンターは必ずしもコーチのようでなくていいのです。打ち解けて話すことができ、あなたにとって何が最善かを常に考えてくれ、信頼できる友のような存在。夢を共有でき、目標や疑問など何を話しても否定せずに聞いてくれる人、それがメンターです。

　誰にとっても必要な存在である大切なメンターを見つけましょう。明日はもうひとりではないと感じられるはずです。

　A mentor is like a friend. It is someone you can trust. A mentor is not necessarily a coach. It is someone you can be open with, someone who has your best interest in mind at all times. Someone who you can share your dreams, aspiration and doubts without any fear of being judged.

　We all need mentor. Find a mentor. Make it a priority. Tomorrow you will not feel lonely.

ダイバーシティ / Diversity

人と違う自分を
大切にしよう

●

Be kind to
yourself

ダイバーシティ / Diversity

　他の人にはない、自分だけの個性を大切にしましょう。それぞれに異なる特徴が多様性を生み、お互いが豊かな経験を得られるのです。

　人と異なるということは、相手が知らない何かをプレゼントできるということ。それがやがて課題を解決したり何かを成し遂げたりする力となり、新たなスタートを踏み出す鍵となるもかもしれません。

　周りの人を豊かにするために、あなたにしかないたくさんの宝物を共有しましょう。そしてそんな自分を思い切り大切にしてあげてくださいね。

　Be kind to the parts of yourself that are different from other people. Our differences bring diversity and enrich our experiences.

　To be different is to have someone new to offer. That something new can be the key to solving a problem, the key to achieving a breakthrough, the key to a new beginning.

　Be kind to yourself. You are full of unique treasures. Be generous. Share them to enrich everyone.

ダイバーシティ / Diversity

多様性を理解する

●

Understand the meaning of diversity

ダイバーシティ / Diversity

　異なる視点や解釈、提案、相容れない意見、不透明な答え……私たちが生きる世界は複雑です。物事が移り変わるめまぐるしさに違和感をおぼえないのであれば、それは感度が鈍っているということかもしれません。

　変化に満ちた日々の中で、周囲のさまざまな意見やアイデアに本当の価値を見出すためには、何度でも繰り返し疑問を持ちましょう。多様性への理解を深めることで洞察力が育まれ、それが課題解決を導く力となるのです。

　We live in a complex world. Conflicting views, conflicting opinions, conflicting interpretations, different approaches and no clear-cut right or wrong answers. Everything moves so fast that it feels that if you are not confused, it means that you are not paying attention.

　Amid a sea of change, ask questions, ask, ask, ask… Seek to understand and find the value in the diversity of thoughts and ideas that are around you. Sensitive to diversity will help you be more insightful. Insight breed understanding and solutions to the problems we face.

ダイバーシティ / **Diversity**

捉え方の違いを
理解する

●

Context changes
everything

ダイバーシティ / Diversity

　あなたは「コンテクスト」とは何か考えたことはありますか？　それは、行動のフレームワークに大きく影響する「物事の背景」や「前後関係」のことです。

　同じ行動でもコンテクストが変われば意味も大きく変わります。だけど私たちは、自分の言動が独立して発生するものだと誤解し、コンテクストの影響力を軽く捉えがちです。

　同じ言動でも視点や立場、状況などによって捉え方がまったく異なるということはよくありますよね。行動する前に、まずは自分を取り巻くコンテクストについてじっくり考えてみましょう。

　Now here is something interesting. Have you ever thought of how important "context" is to everything we do? Context in the framework in which we act.

　Change the context and the same action gains or losses meaning. Human beings constantly underestimate the influence of context. We fall in the trap where we start to believe that our actions are independent from context or that context does not affect us.

　Think again. Depending on various points of view, various situations, various circumstances, the same action is viewed differently. Take the time to understand the context that surrounds you before you take action.

ダイバーシティ / **Diversity**

自分には
バイアスがあると
思うこと

●

Be aware of
your biases

ダイバーシティ / Diversity

　人間の脳は、ハッブル宇宙望遠鏡がこれまで地球に送ってきたデータと同じくらい膨大なデータを、たった30秒で処理するそうです。一度脳に入ったデータは、意識的または無意識的に脳内でファイリングされます。

　自分の脳がファイリングするということは、自分が持つバイアスにかけられるということ。むしろある程度のバイアスがあるからこそ、脳はデータを整理できるといえます。大切なのは、それを意識することで、バイアスによるコントロールを多少なりとも防ぐことができるということです。

　物事を広く見渡せる視野を養い、バイアスの落とし穴にはまらないように注意しましょう。

　The human brain produces in 30 seconds as much data as the Hubble Space Telescope has produced in its lifetime. What happens with data once it enters our brain? The brain organizes it. We have a mental filing system which is both conscious and unconscious.

　It matters to know that we have biases within us. We all do, without exception. The brain could not function without some level of bias. However, if you acknowledge to yourself that you are biased, the bias loses its grip over you.

　You start seeing things with a greater degree of freedom and you can step out of the bias-trap.

Project Quantum メンバーからのメッセージ
Messages from Project Quantum Members

第4章
「自己認識」

Chapter 4
Self-recognition

自己認識 /Self-recognition

"Kill The Parrot!"

●

Kill the Parrot!

自己認識 /Self-recognition

　人は皆頭の中にオウムを飼っています。その内なる声はあなたの自信に疑問を投げかけ、揺さぶりをかけてくることもあるでしょう。すると自分のやるべきことを本当にきちんとできているか不安になるものです。オウムはいつまでも居座り、自分に疑いをかけてしまうような言葉を何度も繰り返すかもしれません。
　でもそんなオウムの声は聞き流して！　自分のことは自分が一番よくわかっています。一生懸命がんばってエネルギーを燃やしてきた自分を信じ、実力を発揮してください。

―――――●―――――

　We all have a parrot inside our heads. That internal voice that questions and shakes your confidence, that parrot repetitive voice that makes you wonder if you are well-prepared or not. The parrot can be persistent, it can keep on saying things that make you doubt yourself.

　KILL THE PARROT! You know what you know. You have put efforts and energy into what you are doing. Believe in yourself and deliver the best performance you are capable of!

自己認識 /Self-recognition

知らなかった自分が
見えてくる

●

Encountering the new you

自己認識 /Self-recognition

　さまざまなことを学んで成長したいという姿勢で努力すれば、必ず素晴らしいことが起こります。努力をするようになるとすぐに自分の変化に気がつき、知らなかった一面が見え始めるのです。それはまるで新しい自分に出会うような感覚であり、エキサイティングでわくわくする体験です。

　これからもずっと学ぶことをやめず、新しい自分を発見し続けてください。

　　When you intently work on your development and continuously strive to learn and grow, something beautiful happens. Soon enough, you start to see and notice that you are changing. Soon enough you start to see a new facet of yourself you did not know. It is like meeting a new part of yourself! It can be exciting and exhilarating.

　　Continue your learning journey and continue discovering the new you.

自己認識/Self-recognition

自分を
モチベートするものを
理解する

●

Understand
what motivates
you

自己認識 /Self-recognition

　自分についてよく知ることは大切なことです。行動、成長、努力を促すものや、役割以上のことをやり抜くモチベーションとなるものを把握するために欠かせません。

　自分自身をじっくりと観察する時間をつくりましょう。現状をどのように見つめているか、課題や新しい状況をどのように捉えているのかなどをメモし、やる気を駆り立てるものを探ってみてください。

　人は皆一人ひとり違います。だからこそ自分についてよく知ることが大切なのです。

　Self-knowledge matters. To know yourself is to understand what makes you tick, what makes you grow, what makes you try harder, what makes you go above and beyond the line of duty.

　Take the time to observe yourself. Take the time to take notes and write down how your mind perceives reality, how your mind deals with challenges and new situations. Take the time to find the fire of motivation that lies within you.

　Everyone is different. Learn to know yourself!

自己認識 /Self-recognition

自分自身を知る
●
Get to know yourself

自己認識 /Self-recognition

　子どものころは多くのことを学習し、新しいことに次々と挑戦したでしょう。人は成長していく過程で、何かを学ぼうとする意欲を失いがちです。日々の仕事やタスクに追われて忙しくなると、自分自身について理解を深めようとすることも忘れてしまいます。

　人は、層がたくさん重なってできた複雑な生き物です。一層ずつはがしていき、その内側にある本当の自分を見つけましょう。自分の能力や可能性について常に好奇心を抱き続けてください。

　When you were a child you studied so many things, you learned so much, you did so many things that were new. As we grow up, somehow we tend to slow down in our learning… we become busy doing things, working on stuff, and somewhere along the way we forget to get to know ourselves.

　We are complex individuals, we are made of many layers. Peel the onion, get to know yourself. Curiosity is a gift that allows you to constantly learn about your capabilities and potential.

自己認識 /Self-recognition

自己の
強み、弱みの
理解

Know your strengths and areas of improvement

自己認識 /Self-recognition

　自分について知ること、コミュニケーション スタイルを築くこと、モチベーションを左右するものを把握するということはとても大切です。得意な分野や強みを活かす方法と同時に、弱みを克服する方法についても考えてみましょう。
　自分についての正しい理解そのものが、強みをのばしたり成長したりするために活用できる、強力な武器へと変わるのです。

　　Just as it is important to know yourself, just as it is important to adjust your communication style, just as it is important to know what motivates you and what bring you down, it is also important to understand what you are good at, your strengths. Know your strengths and you can play to them. Understand where your developmental areas are and you can craft measures to conquer them. Know what you know and know what you do not know.
　　Self-knowledge is a tool that does not betray. Use it to your advantage. Use it to grow.

自己認識 /Self-recognition

自分に合う
マネジメント スタイル
を見つける

Find your own
management
style

自己認識 /Self-recognition

　マネジメント スタイルには、自分の好みや傾向が表れることはあっても、正解か不正解かはありません。リーダー像は誰かのまねである必要はなく、自分なりのリーダーシップを自身が信じるスタイルで育んでいけばいいのです。まさにそれがインクルージョン＆コラボレーションの素晴らしさといえるでしょう。

　自分の可能性に自信を持って。信頼できるスタイルに基づくのが もっとも素晴らしい方法です。あなた自身のスタイルを尊重しましょう。

　There are no rights or wrongs when it comes to style. There are preferences, there are inclinations, but no rights and no wrongs. The leader inside of you need not imitate anyone. You can grow and develop your own authentic leadership, your own authentic style. That is the beauty of inclusion and collaboration.

　Remember to have confidence in your potential. In matters of style, there is no greater good than authenticity. Honor your own.

自己認識 /Self-recognition

リーダーシップ スタイルは 複数持ってよい

●

Believe in adaptive leadership

自己認識 /Self-recognition

　あなたにとってリーダーシップとは何ですか。マネジメントと同じかそれとも別物でしょうか。そして優れたリーダーとマネージャー、それぞれに必要なものは同じか否かという点についても、自分自身に積極的に問いかけてみましょう。きっと最適な答えが見つかるはずです。

　ある人の考えによると、人々がゴールへたどり着けるようにひらめきを与えるのがリーダーで、ゴールへたどり着く方法を見つけられるよう導くのがマネージャーです。さまざまな考え方がありますが、あなたにとってのリーダーシップはたくさんある方法のうちのひとつ。大切なのは、その方法を行動に移してみることで、あなたの内にあるリーダー像を鮮明にすることです。

　今こそ、再び自分自身に問いかけてみてください——リーダーとマネージャーの違いは何だろう？

　What is leadership? Is it the same as management? Are they different? Is what makes a great leader different from what makes a great manager? Think of these things, think of these questions. If you are earnest in your enquiry, you will find the right answers.

　Someone said a leader is the one that inspires people to achieve a goal, while a manager is the one that ensure they know how to get to that goal. Is one right, the other wrong? Your way of leadership, your unique way is one of many. Experiment with it. Try it out. Nurture the leader within you.

　Now think again… What is the difference between a leader and a manager?

自己認識 /Self-recognition

人に与える印象が成果に大きく影響する

The camera is always rolling. Be aware of how you project yourself

自己認識 /Self-recognition

　リーダーシップを身につける過程では、事実や情報を捉える目、自分をアピールする方法、振る舞い方、所作、表情、態度など、たくさんの分野において学びがあることに気づくでしょう。関わりを持つ人たちに与える印象も大切です。

　印象というものは想像以上に人々の記憶に長く残るもの。良い印象を与える効果をどう活用するかが秘訣です。

　自分のイメージやブランド力を駆使しましょう。あなたは自分自身のブランド マネージャーになる最初の一歩を踏み出しています。その能力を存分に活かしてください。

　In your leadership journey, you will find there are many layers of learning. There is the fact, there is the data, there is the way you present and carry yourself, your demeanor, your presence and there is the impression you leave on the people you interact with.

　Now here is a secret. Your impression lingers more than you think. Be mindful of how you come across and use it to deliver better and more impressive results.

　Manage your image, your brand. You are taking the first step to being your own brand manager. Do a great job with it.

自己認識 /Self-recognition

完璧である
必要はない

●

Perfection is
not a virtue

自己認識 /Self-recognition

　自分に対して厳しすぎることはないでしょうか。完璧でないと気が済まない、110％の保障がほしい……そんな風に思っていませんか。

　だけど人生はそううまくはいきません。人生とは常に変化と成長を繰り返し、めまぐるしく進化を遂げる舞台のようなものです。

　今日は完璧にできたけど明日もそうとは限らないのだから、完璧にこだわりすぎる必要はないのです。それよりむしろ精一杯がんばってベストを尽くすことに集中しましょう。

　Sometimes you can be too stern on yourself. You want things to be perfect. You want to have that 110% of security.

　Life does not work that way. Life is a dance of evolution, where things are constantly changing and getting better.

　The perfection of today becomes the imperfection of tomorrow. Do not get too hung up on attaining "perfect". Instead, focus on giving your maximum effort, your best shot, your best self.

自己認識 /Self-recognition

目標を常に見直す

Take the time to set and review your goals

自己認識 /Self-recognition

　こんな言葉があります——計画を立てないのは、失敗する計画を立てているのと同じだ。

　落ち着いてじっくりと考えをめぐらし、年間の目標を書き出してみましょう。少し大胆になって、自分自身の最高の状態を想像し、長年の夢や達成したい課題なども正直に書いてみてください。プライベート、キャリア、メンタル、フィジカルの分野ごとに目標を分類します。書いたものは目につく場所に貼っておき、ゴールを思い出せるようにしましょう。

　そしてときどき見直し、修正したり新たなことを付け加えたりして、ときめく内容にブラッシュ アップしていくのです。目標達成のために実行したことや達成したことを誰かに聞いてもらってください。今度はその人が他の誰かにアイデアを与える存在になるでしょう。

　Someone said "Those who fail to plan, plan to fail".

　Find the inspiration to sit down and write down your personal goals for the year. Be bold. Imagine the very best for yourself, be respectful to your yearnings and aspirations. Categorize them in different areas, personal, professional, mental, physical. Whatever you want to achieve, write it down and put them in places where you can see them and remind you of where you are going.

　Take time to review and adjust them. Make it exciting. Work to achieve your objectives and share with others your own achievements. They will become a source of inspiration for others too!

自己認識 /Self-recognition

心の声を聴く

Listen to your heart

自己認識 /Self-recognition

　何かをやり抜くには、計画したり深く考えたりあるいはスケジュールを管理したりする必要があります。とはいえ、それらは単なる手段にすぎないので、縛られることはありません。思いつくまま行動するための余裕をとっておくことも大切です。

　もし優先順位を変える必要性が出てきたら、心の声に耳を傾けてみてください。そこで方向性を修正した方がいいと感じたならば、その考えに従ってほしい。自分自身の声に正直になるのです。

　人生はダイナミックです。流れにうまく乗っていきましょう。

　Yes, planning, thinking and having a schedule are critical part of a framework to be successful. But at the end of the day, remember that they are just tools that are supposed to serve you, not you serve them. So allow time and space for moments of spontaneity.

　Listen to the voice of your heart if you feel you need to re-prioritize, if you feel you need to adjust course, do so, being true to your own voice.

　Life is dynamic. Follow the flow of life.

自己認識 /Self-recognition

自身を通して
リーダーのあるべき姿
を考える

●

Use yourself as a mirror to find the true image of a leader

自己認識 /Self-recognition

　リーダーシップとは何かということを理解するのは簡単ではありません。優秀なリーダーになるには何をするべきか、リーダーはどのように振る舞うべきか、どのような言動をすべきかについて考えてみましょう。あなたにとっての完璧なリーダー像やロール モデルはありますか？

　自分の考え方や振る舞い方、人との関わり方、何がやる気を出させるか、逆に何が失わせるか、チーム内でできることやできないこと、仕事をどのように仕上げるか、あるいはどのようにしたら失敗するか、よく注意して目を向けてみてください。そうすれば、理想的なリーダーに近づくための要素を見抜くことができるでしょう。それはトライアルを繰り返す旅路のようなものです。

　自分自身について知ることで、自分にとっての真のリーダーシップを見つけてください。

　Leadership is hard to grasp. What is a task to be and become a good leader? How should a leader behave? What is the behavior of a good leader? Is there such a thing as a perfect leader image or role model?

　Being watchful and paying attention to the workings of your own mind, seeing how you behave, how you interact, how you get motivated or de-motivated, how you act or fail to act within your team, how you get work done or fail to get work done, will give you invaluable insights into what is the true role model of a leader. It is a journey, an experiment.

　Find your authentic leadership by learning about yourself.

Project Quantum メンバーからのメッセージ
Messages from Project Quantum Members

第5章
「自信」
「セルフ ブランディング」
「チャンスをつかむ」

Chapter 5
Confidence
Self-branding
Get a chance

自信 / Confidence

もう一歩前に
踏み出す勇気

●

It takes courage
to push forward

自信 / Confidence

　スキルも能力も十分に身につき、そろそろ新しいプロジェクトや仕事に挑戦してみよう……そう思っていても自分自身に疑問を抱き、行動に移せないことがあるでしょう。

　長い間がんばってきたのに、どうして思いとどまってしまうのでしょうか。背中を押してもらうことが必要なときもありますが、とにかく一歩前へ進んだ方がよい場合もあります。

　自分の能力やこれまでの努力を信じましょう。成長は自分を信じることから始まります。一歩を踏み出して前へ進んでいって！

　　　Sometimes, you know you are ready, you know you can do it, you know you have the skills, the capability, the drive to take on a new project, a new job, a new adventure… BUT… you wait, you doubt, you question yourself.

　　　You have worked long and hard... What is stopping you??? Sometimes, we just need a little push. Sometimes all we need is to take one step forward.

　　　Believe in your capabilities, in your efforts to date. You have grown to be where you are by trusting yourself. Take the step! Move ahead!

自信 / Confidence

あなたなら大丈夫

Believe in yourself

自信 / Confidence

　「自信」——それは魔法の言葉。この一言にとてつもない力が込められています。古代ローマの詩人ウェルギリウスの「できると思うから、人は成功するのだ」という言葉のとおり、自信が成功の鍵となるのです。
　リーダーシップを発揮する人はためらうことを知りません。ステップ アップし、自信を持って周囲をリードしていきましょう。

　Confidence. That magic word. Confidence. There is so much strength in that one single word: Confidence. The ancient Roman poet Virgil said it right "They can because they think they can". Confidence is a key.

　Leadership knows no hesitation. Step up and lead, with confidence.

自信 / Confidence

自信がないときこそ
自分を信じよう

●

Believe in your potential, specially when the going gets tough

自信 / Confidence

　疑念が浮かび上がったとき、粘り強さと決意は強力な武器となります。弱さや不安を感じるときこそ、潜在的な能力に意識を向けましょう。内から聞こえてくるささやかな自信の声に耳を傾けてみてください。

　負けないで！　疑念や不安を払拭し、これまでの人生で自分が培ってきた自信を取り戻しましょう。その自信があなたをサポートしてくれるはずです。

　Tenacity and determination are powerful weapons you have at your disposal in moments of doubt. We all have moments of weakness, moments of insecurity, but it is in those very moments that we need to draw on our inner resources and find the small voice of confidence within ourselves.

　Do not let doubt consume you. Consume doubt!!! Consume insecurity. Find the confidence that has led your growth from birth till now. It is here to help you.

自信 / Confidence

自分のペースで進む

Keep your pace

自信 / Confidence

　成長するスピードに決まりなどありません。前進し、進歩し続けることを第一に考え、自分に合ったペースを見つけてください。適したスピードで行動し、自分のタイミングを大切にしましょう。
　きちんと前進していることを実感できると、小さな自信がわき上がってくるものです。自分の成長を楽しんで！

　There are no rules on how fast you must advance. The important thing is to advance, to progress, to continue to evolve. Find your pace. Strike at the right moments. Move at the speed of your choosing. Keep your pace and honor your timing.

　There is a quiet confidence in knowing that you are heading at the right speed. Enjoy the ride!

自信 / Confidence

自分らしく!

●

Be true to yourself

自信 / Confidence

　誰かとそっくりのコピーになる必要はありません。自分らしくありのままの姿で、人とは違う個性を大切にしましょう。
　簡単なことのように感じるかもしれませんが、決められたロール モデルに従ったり合わせたりしなければいけない、というプレッシャーを誰もが感じてしまいがちです。こうしたロール モデルは成功例のひとつにすぎません。惑わされないようにしましょう。
　あなたには未来を切り開く力があるのだから、自分らしくい続けてください。

　Do not become a carbon copy of anyone. Be yourself. Be authentic. Be your own unique self.

　It sounds simple, but many of us feel the pressure to conform, to adjust to some given role model. Do not be confused, those roles models are nothing but things of the past.

　You have the power to create your future. Be yourself.

セルフ ブランディング / Self-branding

女性らしさ
ではなく
女性ならでは

●

Your diversity is much more than just being a woman

セルフ ブランディング / Self-branding

　あなたが持つ多様性や高い能力は、女性らしさとはまた別です。あなたは女性として全体を捉える視点を備えています。その多様性によって人々に貢献できることに自信を持ち、最善を尽くしてください。そうすれば、周りはあなたのリーダーシップを歓迎し、さらに発揮できるようサポートしてくれるでしょう。

　The diversity you bring to the table, what you can contribute is independent of your perceived femininity. As a woman, you have a point of view that help complement the whole. Have confidence in what your diversity can contribute. Bring out the best you have to offer and the world will welcome your leadership and help you expand the gifts you bring.

セルフ ブランディング / Self-branding

ノートを取るな

●

Do not take the back seat

セルフ ブランディング / Self-branding

　ミーティングに出席するときは前方の席に座りましょう。誰かが話していることを静かにノートを取るだけの人にはならないでください。地位や役職にかかわらず、どんな場面でもリーダーシップは発揮できるもの。活発に参加できるよう自分の背中を押してあげてください。何かしら貢献できるものを持っているなら、それを前面に出しましょう。
　「ノートを取る」か「率先してミーティングに参加する」かの選択では、いつも後者を選んでくださいね。

　When you attend meetings with others, take the front seat. Do not be the one who is always quiet just taking notes while others do the talk. Leadership exists in every moment, regardless of position or title. Bring yourself forward, actively participate. Remember you have something to contribute, you must bring it forward.

　In the choice between "taking notes" and "leading a meeting", always choose to lead.

セルフ ブランディング / Self-branding

スタイルは変わる、変えられる

You evolve and change constantly. Use it to your advantage

セルフ ブランディング / Self-branding

　物事には変えられないこともあります。でもスタイルは変えることができるのです。

　自分自身のスタイルや人に与える印象、映り方、コミュニケーション スタイルなどは進化させることができますし、やがて進化していくものでしょう。注意力、集中力、決断力はすべてスタイルを変化させるのに不可欠な要素です。例えば大学時代からの自分を振り返ってみてください。話し方は同じでも、物事の提示の仕方や説明の仕方は成長しているのではないでしょうか。

　経験が有意義で大切なものであると同時に、成長のための計画的な努力やトレーニングもまた大きな変化をもたらします。さらに向上し、最高のビジョンを実現させましょう。

　　Few things are fixed. Few things do not change much. But style, is not one of them.

　　Your style, the way you come across, how you project yourself and your overall communication style can and will evolve. Attention, focus and determination are critical in making changes and adjustments to your style. Look back and see how much you have changed since you were a student at university for example. You do talk the same way, you do not present or explain things in the same manner.

　　Experience matters and helps, but deliberate practice, deliberate effort to improve can bring about major changes too. Aim high. Realize your best vision.

セルフ ブランディング / Self-branding

セルフ ブランディング
は常に意識すべき

●

Self-branding
matters

セルフ ブランディング / Self-branding

　オフィスに行けば誰かに会います。ミーティングに出ればお客様を迎えます。デスクに座れば打ち合わせの電話がかかってくることもあるでしょう。過ぎゆく一日の中で、あなたはずっとパーソナル ブランドを身にまとっています。それは発する言葉や態度、表情、立ち振る舞い、指示の出し方、沈黙しているときにさえ表れるものです。

　一度立ち止まってセルフ ブランディングを意識してみましょう。自分を押さえつけて演じるのではなく、周囲を注意深く見つめながらベストの自分でのぞむことが大切です。

　You go to the office, you meet people, you go to meetings, you meet customers, you sit at your desk and get on conference calls. A day goes by and throughout the whole time you carry your personal brand with you. It comes through in your words, in your posture, in how you carry yourself, in your command skills, in your eloquence or silence.

　Take time to pause and be aware of your self-branding. This does not mean you need to put yourself in a box and go pretend be something you are not. It does mean that you are alert and always ready to project the best version of you.

チャンスをつかむ / Get a chance

チャンスに
「次」はない

●

Some
opportunities
come only once

チャンスをつかむ / Get a chance

　最高のチャンスが訪れたなら、それがもたらす可能性について思いをめぐらせましょう。今しかないという思いで飛びつく勢いも大切です。行動的になるには思い込みも必要。チャンスは二度訪れるとは限らないのです。

　When a great opportunity comes to you... it is time for you to sit down and reflect. Have a certain sense of urgency to jump on things that will make you grow. Be biased toward action-orientation. Sometimes opportunities do not come twice.

チャンスをつかむ / Get a chance

準備を怠らない

Be ready

チャンスをつかむ / Get a chance

　抜擢の機会は突然訪れるかもしれません。だからこそ、準備を怠らないことに大きな価値があります。それは、次のステップに進む準備、あるいはリーダーになるための準備ができているということを、周囲に知らせるシグナルともなります。

　リーダーへとステップ アップするために準備は欠かせません。日常業務を超えた課題に挑戦したりプロジェクトに参加したりすることで、新しい経験や知識をたくわえて万全の状態を保ちましょう。いつでも自分自身の準備を怠らないで！

　Unexpected Promotion might come suddenly, that's why it is important and meaningful to continue preparing for your chance. It signals to the world that you are ready for more, that you are ready to lead.

　Stepping up in leadership needs readiness. Prepare yourself through stretch assignments and new projects. Prepare yourself through new experiences and new learning. Prepare yourself and be ready!

チャンスをつかむ / Get a chance

質問する習慣を
身につける

Ask questions

チャンスをつかむ / Get a chance

　あなたは子どものころ、頭が良いとか物知りだなどと褒められませんでしたか。やがて新しいことを発見して広い世界を知るようになると、誰かに質問することはなくなり、すぐに物知りではなくなってしまうものです。

　知恵、スキル、知識は、疑問を投げかける人に与えられるもの。最終的には、好奇心に満ちあふれた人が物事に精通した人になるのです。常に疑問を持つことを忘れず、もっと知りたい、もっとやってみたいという探究心を抱き続けてください。また周りの人もそのように導いてあげましょう。

　When I was a child, someone told me I was smart. When I was a child someone told me I knew so much. After that happened, I heard new things, I saw new worlds and I stopped asking questions. Not after long, I ended up knowing less than others.

　Wisdom, skills and knowledge come to those who ask questions. The curious ones win in the battle for mastery. Utilize your inquisitive mind to learn and do more. Never stop, always question and lead others to do the same.

CISCOの女性リーダー❶

佐藤菜穂子氏 (Naoko Sato)

シスコシステムズ合同会社
コーポレート事業統括
法人ビジネス事業部
バーチャル・セールスマネージャー

コンフォートゾーンを飛び出す
一瞬の躊躇はあっても、挑戦する

育休明けには、テレワーク環境を有効活用

　1998年、私は大学を卒業して社会人になりました。以後の12年間、日本企業と米系企業の2社で主に営業畑の仕事をしました。

　印象に残っているのは、米系企業に移って5年目ごろの出来事です。当時の日本法人社長が次世代リーダー育成の一環として、社長をはじめとするエグゼクティブの業務を間近で見て学べるよう1年交代で若手の社員を経営企画室で就業させていました。私にも声がかかり、社長の任期が満了するまでの9ヵ月と短い期間でしたが、組織の運営や会計的な知識を学ぶきっかけになりました。

　シスコに入社したのは、2010年のことです。以前、一緒に仕事をした知り合いがシスコで働いていて、その方から「応募してみたら」

と声をかけてもらったのです。

そろそろ、この会社に入ってから6年が過ぎようとしています。2015年9月までの5年余りはパートナー事業部に在籍し、パートナー（販売代理店）向けの営業プログラム開発やセミナーの企画、運営などに携わりました。この間、プライベートでは出産というイベントがあり、育休を含めて半年強の休みをとりました。

育休明け、特にありがたいと思ったのはテレワーク環境です。子どもが病気をしたときなど、ときどき在宅で仕事をしました。その後、在宅勤務の頻度は徐々に落としていきました。

一般に、テレワーク環境を用意している企業は少なくありませんが、それだけでは不十分だと思います。仕組みとあわせて、利用者と職場にテレワークを受け入れる文化がなければ、有効活用されることはないでしょう。シスコのように仕組みと文化の両方が揃っている企業は、日本ではあまり多くないように思います。

「部下を持つマネージャー職」へのチャレンジ

育休を終えて自分なりに仕事のペースがつかめたころ、現在のポジションに応募してみないかと声をかけられました。バーチャル・セールスという営業チームのマネージャーです。

パートナー事業部での仕事はシスコの国内外の人たちとコミュニケーションをとりながら、さまざまなリソースを組み合わせてパートナーに提供するといったものでした。業務を通じて多くのことを学びましたが、同事業部で5年を経過するころには「次のステップに進みたい」という気持ちが芽生えていました。応募した後、幸い希望どおりのポジションに就くことができました。

正直にいうと、迷いはありました。大きな理由は、部下を持つマ

ネージャー職の経験がなかったことです。なおかつ、お客様を担当し、お客様に紐付く営業的なターゲットを持つ仕事もシスコでは経験したことがありませんでした。「本当に自分にできるだろうか」という不安は大きかったので、自分では思い切った決断をしたと思っています。

3年、5年と同じ部門にいれば業務の経験値も高まり、それなりの自信ができてきます。実際にやっている仕事を離れて、できるかどうかわからない別の仕事に移るときには、多くの人が一瞬のためらいを感じるのではないでしょうか。

私自身を振り返ると、シスコへの入社を決めたとき、マネージャーに応募したとき、大事な場面ではコンフォートゾーン（居心地のいい場所）を飛び出すことを選んできました。その選択が自分のキャリアをつくってきたと感じています。

バーチャル・セールスは内勤営業のチームで、電話をはじめさまざまなコミュニケーションツールを使ってお客様に対する提案活動を行っています。担当するお客様は大企業から中小規模の企業までさまざまです。お客様との直接的なつながりを大事にしていますが、製品の提案や販売に際してはパートナーとの協業が欠かせません。

チームのメンバーは13人。チームを率いる者として心掛けているのは、メンバーが快適に働けるような環境を整えることです。業務を阻害する要因にできるだけ早く気づき、取り除くことが大事な役割です。

例えば、メンバーに困りごとがあれば、解答を持っていそうな誰かに橋渡しする、あるいは業務を改善するための気づきを与える。そんなマネージャーでありたいと思っています。

同じような悩みを抱えた仲間がいた

　Project Quantumには十数名の女性とともに参加し、1年近くの間に何度か集まって、リーダーシップやコミュニケーションについて学びました。「リーダーはこうあるべき」と身構える必要は必ずしもなくて、自分なりのスタイルを見つけていけばいい。プロジェクトでのさまざまな活動を通じて、そんな気づきをもらったように思います。

　印象的だったのは、劇団俳優によるコミュニケーションのトレーニングです。いまもミーティングなどの場で、そのときの指導を思い出して、どんな言動がふさわしいだろうかと考えたりします。

　最大の収穫は、参加したメンバーとの出会いです。研修などの中で一緒に話す機会が多く、率直な対話を通じて、同じような悩みを抱えた仲間がいることを知りました。これから仕事を続けていく中で、お互いに励まし合い、知恵を出し合いながらよりよい関係を築いていきたいと願っています。

　シスコはグローバルな組織であり、多様な組織です。日本法人で働く海外出身者も多い。逆に、日本から海外のオフィスに移って働く人もいます。例えば、私の知っている入社2年目の女性は、先ごろオーストラリアに異動しました。どこかの国のポジションで人材が必要になれば、世界規模でオープンな募集が行われます。

　その女性も自ら手を挙げて、現在のポジションに就くことができました。今後、彼女のような人たちが日本に戻ってくれば、職場の多様性はもっと高まるでしょう。多様性が価値を生み出す職場づくりに、私自身も貢献していきたいと思っています。

CISCO Women Leaders❶

Jump out of your comfort zone
Even if you have a momentary
hesitation, take the challenge.

Naoko Sato
Virtual Sales Manager
Corporate Business Supervisor
Corporate Business Division
Cisco Systems G.K

Effective use of Teleworking environment during maternity leave

In 1998, I graduated from university and became a working adult. For the next 12 years, I primarily worked in the sales field in both Japanese and U.S. companies.

I clearly remember an incident that happened in the fifth year after I started working at the American company. As a part of the next generation leader's training, young employees were given the opportunity to work in the management planning office for one year taking turns, so that they could observe and learn about the jobs of the president and executives. I was also assigned which lasted only for nine months until president's term ended. I learned about management and gained financial and accounting knowledge, which was very valuable.

I joined Cisco Systems in 2010. Earlier, an acquaintance with whom I had previously worked was working at Cisco, and they suggested that I should try applying at Cisco.

And now I have been working at this company for over six years. For a period of over five years, until September 2015, I was in the Partner Division and had worked in business program development and planning, and in managing seminars for the partners (distributors). During that period, I took personal leave for six months including my maternity leave.

When I returned from my maternity leave, I was grateful for the teleworking environment, which enabled me to work from home when my child was sick. After that, I gradually reduced the amount of telecommuting.

There are quite a few companies out there who have a teleworking environment setup, but I do not think that is enough. Teleworking cannot be used effectively unless the user and workplace accommodate the teleworking culture along with the company structure. I think Japan has very few companies like Cisco Systems where both the teleworking technology and company culture go hand in hand.

The Challenges of managing subordinates

When the maternity leave was over and I was catching up with the pace of work, I was encouraged to apply for this position. I am the manager of the sales team known as Virtual Sales.

My job in the Partner Division was to communicate with domestic and overseas people at Cisco Systems and at the same time provide the partners with combinations of various resources. I got to learn a lot of things at that job, but after working in the same division for five years,

I strongly felt that I should move to the next step. I applied and fortunately I was able to get the position I wanted.

Honestly, I was not sure. The main reason is I did not have experience managing subordinates. In addition, it was the first time I had to deal with customers and with sales that were directly linked to gaining customers at CISCO. I was very anxious as to whether I would be able to do this, but I took the plunge and made my decision.

If you work in the same department for three years or five years, the value of your experience increases and you become self-confident. When people leave their current job and change to another one that they are unsure about, there must be a momentary hesitation.

When I look back at myself, at the time when I decided to join Cisco Systems, and at the time when I applied for the manager's position, I have come this far by choosing to jump out of my comfort zone at important points in my life. I feel that these choices made my career.

Virtual sales is the in-house sales team and we provide support to the customers using telephone and other communication tools. Our clients include major corporations and small to mid-size. Direct connection with the client is important, but collaboration with partners is essential when proposing and marketing our products.

My team consists of 13 members. As a team leader my aim is to create an environment where members can work comfortably. Recognizing as early as possible the primary factors that can harm the business and eliminating them is an important duty.

For example, if a member is experiencing a problem, I am the bridge to the person with the solution, or I help them focus on improving the business. I wish to continue being this kind of a manager.

I had a colleague who had similar concerns

I participated in Project Quantum with about 10 women. We met several times for nearly a year and learned about leadership and communication. It is not necessary to feel that a leader should behave in certain way. It is better to find one's own style. I believe that through the various project activities my awareness increased.

Communication training given by a theater actor was quite impressive. Even now in the meetings and other scenarios, I recall that coaching and think about what kind of language and behavior would be appropriate.

The biggest takeaway for me was getting to meet the other participants. During the training, there were opportunities to have discussions. During the direct interactions I realized that the others were having similar problems. When we continue with our work after this, I hope that we build even better relationships while encouraging one another and sharing know-how.

Cisco Systems is a global organization and has diverse structures. Many foreign graduates are working in Japanese corporations. On the other hand, there are many Japanese people who have moved to overseas offices. For example, a woman I know who joined our company two years ago has been transferred to Australia. If a capable person is required for any position in any country, an open recruitment is performed on a global scale.

In this instance, the woman showed her willingness to take up the opportunity and was appointed to her current assignment. In future, when people like her return to Japan, workplace diversity will increase further. I also wish to contribute to creating a workplace where diversity adds value.

CISCOの女性リーダー❷

山田晴香氏（Haruka Yamada）

シスコシステムズ合同会社
テクニカルサービス
カスタマーインタラクションネットワーク
プロダクトマネージャー

エンジニアからの方向転換、自分に何ができるかを考えた

メンターやスポンサーに助けられて

　大学を卒業後、2004年にシスコに入社しました。文系学部出身ですが、エンジニアになりたいと思い、入社後がむしゃらに技術と格闘しました。同期入社のエンジニアたちは技術が大好きで、知識量も多く能力も高い。そんな同期の仲間に、圧倒される気持ちでした。そこで、2年半後に方向転換しました。自分に何ができるだろうと考えて、エンジニアとしての業務に加えて、作業手順書の更新などを自主的に行っていると、そんな自分を見てくれていた方から、「今度、オペレーションのチームを立ち上げるんだけど、やってみない？」と誘われました。

　こうして2007年に、オペレーション部門へと異動。お客様の機器で障害が発生したとき、技術支援を提供するテクニカルサポートチー

ムが、一貫して高い品質のサービスを提供できるようなプロセス策定や改善などを行う仕事です。自分に合っていたのか、楽しく、やりがいを感じて働くことができました。

　オペレーション部門で4年半が過ぎたころ、今度はテクノロジー部門のマネージャーになってほしいと声がかかりました。技術の現場をいったん離れており、初めて部下を持つことへの不安感もあって、自分としては断るつもりで「ムリです」というと、上司からは「この会社に、チャレンジしない人材はいらない」と喝を入れられました。スポンサーや周囲からの温かい励ましもあって、結局はチャレンジすることに。それが、2011年のことです。

　当初は、エンジニアの道を離れた自分に技術チームのマネージャーが務まるだろうかと不安でいっぱいでしたが、ポストテクニカルサポート部門のマネージャー職としては、3年半ほど仕事をしました。その間に、10人ほどだった部下の数は倍近くに増えました。

部下を持って気づいたフェアネスの重要性

　この3年半は、社会人になってから最も成長を実感できた時期です。

　部下は全員男性で、ほとんどが自分よりも年上でした。マネージャーとしてやってきた私を見て、みんなは驚いたと思います。自分の役割として、業務上の課題を見つけて改善し、エンジニアが仕事をしやすい環境を整えることに努めました。前の部署で、プロセス改善に取り組んだ経験が役立ちました。あるプロセスの見直しを行って実際に成果が出てからは、周囲からもマネージャーとして認められるようになったと感じられるようになりました。

　マネージャーとしての試行錯誤の中で学んだことは、フェアネス

195

の重要性です。チームには様々な個性を持つメンバーがいます。それぞれの強みを生かすことも重要ですが、同時に、各メンバーと公平に接することを心掛けました。

とてもやりがいのある仕事でしたが、もう少し経験の幅を広げたいという気持ちもあって、2015年に別の業務を希望しました。コンタクトセンターの運営部門で、現在も、そのオペレーションマネージャーとして活動しています。

コンタクトセンターを統括するのは、シスコのグローバル組織です。上司や同僚の多くは外国人という多様性に富む環境です。その中で、私の仕事はコンタクトセンター業務をデザインすること。例えば、新しいサービスを提供するとき、コンタクトセンターはどう対応すべきか、どんなサポートが必要になるのかを考え、それを現場の業務に落とし込んでいきます。

私が担当しているのは国内とフィリピン、コスタリカのコンタクトセンターです。時差や商習慣の違いに戸惑うこともありましたが、新しい働き方の工夫もできます。時差についていえば、早朝や夜中にビデオ会議が入ることもしばしばですが、テレワーク環境を使えば十分対応することができます。例えば、早朝自宅でビデオ会議をすませ、午前中は在宅で勤務した後、昼ごろ出社するとか。働き方については任されているので、自分のペースで仕事をしています。

改めて気づいた自信を持つことの重要性

Project Quantumへの参加という話を聞いたとき、正直にいうと「ありがたい」という思いと、「なぜ女性だけ、このようなトレーニングを受けるのか」という疑問が相半ばする状態でした。しかし、実際に参加して自己認識に変化が生まれ、キャリアのターニングポイン

トとなりました。また、多様性のある組織づくりや多様性に基づく価値創造を推進するうえで、女性向けのリーダーシップトレーニングは必要だと感じるようになりました。

Project Quantumのメニューの1つに、能力開発トレーニングがありました。自分を知り、他者を知り、その上でいかに自分を表現するかといった内容です。特にインパクトがあったのは、自己表現について。私たちが行うプレゼンに対して、プロフェッショナルな表現者である俳優の先生から何度もダメ出しがありました。

プレゼンターの自信のないしぐさや雰囲気を、相手は敏感に感じとるものです。そんな指導を受けながら、自信が相手に伝わるプレゼンができるまでやり直しが続きました。自信を持つことの重要性に、改めて気づくことができました。

トレーニングで学んだことは業務の中で実践しています。先日、フィリピンのコンタクトセンターに出張したときのことです。初めて会う人たちとの英語でのコミュニケーションを考えると、どうしても不安になります。でも、日本では何度も経験してきたこと。そう思って「心配ない、大丈夫」と自分に言い聞かせました。できるだけリラックスするよう心掛けてワークショップに臨んだところ、満足できる成果を得ることができました。

経験を自信へと上手に変換しながら、この先もチャレンジを続けていきたいです。

197

When I took a step away from engineering, I wondered what my capabilities were.

Haruka Yamada
Product Manager
Customer Interaction Network
Technical Services
Cisco Systems G.K

And I had a mentor.

After graduation, I joined Cisco Systems in 2004. I had graduated from the Faculty of Policy Studies but I wanted to become an engineer. After joining the company, I worked hard to learn the technology. The engineers who had joined the company with me loved technology. Therefore, they had a lot of knowledge about it and were more capable. I was overwhelmed by having colleagues like them. Then, after two and half years I changed my

course. In addition to my regular job as an engineer,
I voluntarily reviewed and upgraded operations manuals on my own to explore my potential. At that time my mentor told me that they were starting an Operation team and asked if wanted to join in.

In this way, I shifted to the Operation department in 2007. The job of the operations team is to help improve operational excellence and quality of technical support team that delivers troubleshooting assistance to customer. Maybe because the job was a good fit for me, I enjoyed it and I started feeling like the job was worthwhile.

After around four and half years in the Operations department, the supervisor wanted me to become the manager of the Technical department. I had been away temporarily from the technology and was very nervous because I would be managing subordinates for the first time.

I thought it would be impossible for me and wanted to reject the offer. But then my boss gave me push saying "We do not need a person who does not take challenges." Because of the support and encouragement from the people around me, I finally decided to accept the offer. That was in 2011.

I worked as manager in the Post-Technical Support Department for three and half years though I was not confident about managing a technical team after the setback during my engineering career. At the beginning, I had nearly 10 subordinates, and soon the number doubled.

I realized the importance of "Fairness" from my subordinates

This three and a half years as a manager was a significant change in my career and my personal development.

All my subordinates were men and almost all of them were senior to me. I think all were surprised to see me as a manager. My role was to identify and improve the issues in the work and to prepare a favorable environment for engineers. My experience with "process improvement," which I had gained from the previous department was useful for me. After getting the actual results of the process review, the colleagues working around me accepted me as a manager.

What I learned from my trial and error as a manager is "fairness". In a team, every member has a different personality. I learned to encourage the strength of the members and at the same time be impartial with all the members.

Although I enjoyed working there as a manager in technical team, I also wanted to broaden my experience in other fields. Therefore I decided to transfer to another department in 2015. Now I am working as an Operation manager at the Contact Center Department.

Cisco Contact Center is managed by the global organization. The environment of this department is diverse, since many of my seniors and colleagues are non-Japanese. My job is to design the operations at the Contact Center. For example, when we are going to provide a new service, I think about how the Contact Center should handle it, what kind of support is necessary and how to apply it to the on-site work.

I support Contact Centers in Japan, Philippines, and Costa Rica. There are times when I get a little confused due to the time difference and differences in commercial culture, but trying to accept diversity and work as one team. Due to the time differences, I sometimes have to take video conferences early in the morning or late at night, but the Teleworking environment enables me to handle them very well. For example, I can go to the office at noon after completing the video conference that started in the early morning at home. I am doing my work at my own pace because it is up to me to work out how to get it done.

Importance of Self-Confidence

When I heard that I was going to participate in Project Quantum, honestly, I felt pleased but at the same time I wanted to ask that "Why do only women need to take such training?" But participating in the training program proved to be extremely valuable for me. My level of self-confidence changed, which provided a turning point in my career.

Additionally, I felt we need leadership training for female to accelerate diverse organization and value creation from diversity.

Among the tasks in "Project Quantum," there was one task named "Capability Development." The task included points like first knowing yourself and others and then deciding how to act. Self-expression had a particular impact on me. During our presentations, the professional instructors, who were professional actors, were often pointing out our faults.

Audiences can sense a presenter's lack of confidence and other feelings. Under the guidance of the instructors, we continued to redo our presentations until we could communicate our self-confidence to the audience. I realized once again the importance of having confidence.

I am applying the points that I have learned in the training to day-to-day work. I recently visited the Philippines Contact Center on a business trip. I needed to host a workshop in English with the people I've met for the first time there. This situation was enough to make myself nervous, but I know that I have experienced this types of workshop many times in Japan. So I told myself "Don't worry! Everything will be all right!" I tried to relax as much as possible and when I run the workshop, and everything was fine.

I would like to continue taking challenging opportunities by converting my experiences into self-confidence.

Annella Heytens
アネラ ハイテン

Vice President,
Human Resources APJC
Cisco

エピローグ

　10年ほど前のことです。ある会社での会議中、私は出ていきたくてたまらなくなりました。その会議のメンバーになるために10年以上も必死に働いてきたにもかかわらずです。睡眠時間を削り、何時間も残業し、昇進するために他のすべてのことを犠牲にし、なにがなんでもトップに昇りつめたいという思いを実現させました。でもあの重役会議室に座っているときに、私は気づいてしまったのです。好きでもない人たちと同じ会議室に座るために、自分はがむしゃらに働いてきたのだと。

　一体なぜこんなところに来てしまったのだろう？　グレーのスーツに身を包み、利益を上げて、いくつものプロジェクトを回すことに長けてはいても、自分の部下のマネージメントが下手な人たちと一緒に並ぶために？　そう疑問に思ったことがすべてのターニング ポイントになりました。私はその会議室にいる人たちが気に入らなかっただけでなく、自分のことも好きではなくなってしまったのです。

その後まもなく会社を辞め、シスコに転職しました。給料が
減ることなど気になりませんでした。

　この本には、シスコで実際に働く女性たちからのアドバイス
がつまっています。自己を変革すること、自己を知ること、自
信を築くこと、ステップ アップすること、居心地の良い状態か
ら一歩踏み出すこと、難題に挑むこと、自分をブランド化する
こと、思い切って率先すること。これらの教訓を心に刻めば、
みなさんもきっと成功を手にして人生を変えることができるで
しょう。

　男性社会の中で女性がトップに昇りつめるには、男性のよう
にアグレッシブで、常に動きまわり、競争心がなければ無理だ
と思っていました。でもその結果、私は私ではなくなってしまっ
たのです。10 年間の努力の末に実現させた自分を好きになれま
せんでした。

Annella Heytens
アネラ ハイテン

Vice President,
Human Resources APJC
Cisco

　私の場合、それに気づくのに何年もかかってしまいました。
「自分以外の誰か」になる必要などなかったのです。ありのまま
の自分でトップまで昇りつめるのは無理、という考えはただの
幻想です。「男勝り」になる必要はありません。操り人形になる
必要もなければ、スーパー ウーマンを演じる必要もないので
す。女性だから不利だと感じるべきではなく、むしろそれを積
極的に利用しましょう。女性であることを受け容れて、不利を
有利に変えるのです。この本を読んで、みなさんにも私と同じ
気づきを得てほしいと思います。

　自分の強さに目を向けて真のリーダーシップを発揮してくだ
さい。そのパワフルな個性と自然なスタイルに、周囲の人たち
はポジティブなリアクションや応援を返してくれるでしょう。
自分を偽って信念を曲げたり競争したりする必要はありません。
女性として自分の得意分野を活かせば、秀でることは可能なの
です。

Epilogue

It is almost ten years ago that I sat in a company meeting and couldn't wait to make it out the door. I'd determinedly worked for over a decade to sit in that meeting. I had lost sleep, put in the hours at the office and focused solely on getting ahead, at the exclusion of all else. I had a dead-set resolve to make it to the top. And I did. But sitting in that board room, I realized I had worked so hard to sit in a room with people I did not even like.

It was a turning point: holy cow, how did I get here? In this grey suit, surrounded by people who were excellent at gaining business and juggling projects, but terrible at managing their own employees? Not only did I dislike the people in the room, I no longer even liked myself anymore.

Not long after that moment, I quit my job and joined Cisco. I even took a pay cut.

Annella Heytens
アネラ ハイテン

Vice President,
Human Resources APJC
Cisco

This book is filled with advice from real Cisco women. Lessons on transformation, self-knowledge, building confidence, stepping up, venturing out of your comfort zone, embracing challenges, self-branding, being bold and daring to lead. It is amazing material that will lead you to succeed and make a real difference in your life if you take it to heart.

I hope you do the same with my experience. As a woman climbing up the ladder towards making partner, I thought I had to be just like my male peers: aggressive, driven, competitive. It turned out that that was not who I was. And as a result, I did not like who I had worked 10 years to become.

It took me years to realize that you don't have to be anyone other than who you are. The idea that you can not make it to the top without destroying yourself is an illusion, plain and simple. There is no reason to 'man up'. You did not have to become a puppet or pretend to be a super woman. You should not feel like you are disadvantaged because you are female - in fact make use of it! Take your limitations, and turn them to your advantage.

Focus on your strengths and authentic leadership. This powerful individuality, this natural style, is what the people around you will respond to with positivity and cheer. You do not have to sell out or compete like someone you are not. Center on what you are good at as a female and you will excel.

おわりに

　あなたは何らかの理由があってこの本を手に取っていることでしょう。これらのメッセージがあなたに最高の価値をもたらし、リーダーシップを探求する旅路において新たな可能性やチャンスへの扉を開くことを願っています。実際にブレークスルーを起こすのは、この本を閉じた後のあなたです。

これから何をしますか。
どんな人になりたいですか。
どれほどの成長を目指しますか。
その答えを知っているのは、あなた自身です。

Final message

You found this book or maybe this book found you for a reason. The message in these pages only wants the best for you. The message in these pages seeks to open a new world of possibilities and opportunities in your own leadership journey. The real magic happens after you close this book.

What will you do?
What will you be?
How high will you fly?
Only you know the answer to that.

謝　辞

本書の制作にあたり、以下の皆様には並ならぬ尽力をいただきました。

ここにお名前を記し、改めて感謝の意を表します。

Project Quantum 第一期メンバー

Francine Katsoudas（Cisco Systems）

Shari Slate（Cisco Systems）

Janet Ramey（Cisco Systems）

Annella Heytens（Cisco Systems）

Christian Barrios（シスコシステムズ合同会社）

Tom Browne（シスコシステムズ合同会社）

宮薗 妙子（シスコシステムズ合同会社）

岡本 真理（シスコシステムズ合同会社）

Project Quantum
Member Profile

第一期Project Quantumで
1年間に学んだことを、
本書の60のメッセージにまとめた13人のメンバー

長崎 友美　Yumi Nagasaki
- **部署と役職　Section and position**
  グローバル サービス プロバイダー事業部
  シニア アカウント マネージャー
  Senior Account Manager
  Global Service Provider
- **入社年　Employed since**　　　　2007

仕事のポリシー　My work policy
要望をきちんと捉えて日本の市場を本社に伝えるなど、相手の視点に立って考える。

To consider things according to someone else's perspective, such as by understanding the customer's needs correctly and communicating the Japanese market to HQ.

吉田 留津子　Rutsuko Yoshida
- **部署と役職　Section and position**
  アドバンスド サービス
  クロス ファンクショナル
  プロジェクト マネージャー
  Cross-functional Project Manager
  Advanced Services
- **入社年　Employed since**　　　　2010

座右の銘　Personal motto
「人間にとって、その人生は作品である」。安易な決断はせず、ありたい自分を大事にする。

"For a human being, life itself is work." I wish to forego easy decisions, and respect the image of myself that I aspire to.

上野 由美　Yumi Ueno
- **部署と役職　Section and position**
  コラボレーション アーキテクチャ事業部
  セールス ビジネス ディベロップメント マ
  ネージャー
  Sales Business Development Manager
  Collaboration Architecture
- **入社年　Employed since**　　　　2001

これからチャレンジしたいこと　In the future
子どもが成長したら、海外でMBAを取得したい。

When my daughters grown up, I want to challenge MBA abroad.

吉澤 浩美　Hiromi Yoshizawa
- **部署と役職　Section and position**
  テクニカル サービス
  シニア マネージャー
  Senior Manager
  Technical Servicesr
- **入社年　Employed since**　　　　2006

シスコの好きなところ Why do you like Cisco?
権限を持たせてもらえるので、緊張感の中でもリラックスして仕事ができるところ。

Since the company gives me some authority, I can work in a relaxed manner even when there's tension.

千田 恭子　Kyoko Senda
- **部署と役職　Section and position**
  APJC ビジネス パートナーシップ
  ビジネス オペレーション マネージャー
  Business Operation Manager
  APJC Business Partnership
- **入社年　Employed since**　2000

休日の過ごし方　On your day off
ホット ヨガを 2 年ほど続けているほか、首や肩が凝るので整体に行く。

I have been doing hot yoga for two years, and also go to manipulative treatment for my stiff neck and shoulders.

平田 絵　Kai Hirata
- **部署と役職　Section and position**
  エンタープライズ事業部
  シニア アカウント マネージャー
  Senior Account Manager
  Enterprise Sales
- **入社年　Employed since**　2001

仕事のポリシー　My work policy
Challenge and Execution。常にチャレンジと実行を重ねて、変化への対応と成長を目指していく。

Always taking a new challenge and taking into action so that I can lead the change and grow myself.

田名部 朋子　Tomoko Tanabe
- **部署と役職　Section and position**
  パブリック セクター事業部
  シニア アカウント マネージャー
  Senior Account Manager
  Public Sector Sales
- **入社年　Employed since**　2005

座右の銘　Personal motto
「Where there is a will, there is a way」。強い思いはいつか実現する。

"Where there is a will, there is a way." I wish to engage myself in anything with a strong passion.

田村 亜弓　Ayumi Tamura
- **部署と役職　Section and position**
  マーケティング本部
  マーケティング マネージャー
  Marketing Manager
  Marketing
- **入社年　Employed since**　2005

シスコの好きなところ　Why do you like Cisco?
ビジネス リーダーとして業界へ発信し続ける姿勢、社員が挑戦したいことを受け止める文化。

Demonstrating thought leadership to the industry. A culture which welcome employees to challenge themselves.

佐藤 麻子　Asako Sato
- **部署と役職　Section and position**
  サービス営業部
  プログラム マネージャー
  Program Manager
  Service Sales
- **入社年　Employed since**　2010

これからチャレンジしたいこと　In the future
断捨離。自分にとって必要かどうかを考えて物を整理することは心の整理にもつながる。

"Dan sha ri" (decluttering). Organizing my belongings by thinking about whether I need each object to help me better organize my mind well.

原田 慶子　Keiko Harada
- **部署と役職　Section and position**
  マーケティング本部
  マーケティング マネージャー
  Marketing Manager
  Marketing
- **入社年　Employed since**　2013

シスコの好きなところ　Why do you like Cisco?
組織にとってよい方向性などを話し合って進められる、型がなく自由なところ。

I can discuss a good program or tactic for the organization when doing my work. There is not rigid formality but freedom.

前原 朋実　Tomomi Maehara

●部署と役職　**Section and position**
エンタープライズ ネットワーキング事業部
プロダクト マネージャー
Product Manager
Enterprise Networking Division
●入社年　**Employed since**　　　2002

休日の過ごし方　　On your day off

日本人に馴染みのない場所への海外旅行、海外ドラマの鑑賞、久しぶりにピアノを復活中。

Overseas travel to locations unfamiliar to most Japanese, watching foreign dramas, and playing piano which I started again after a long break.

佐藤 菜穂子　Naoko Sato

●部署と役職　**Section and position**
コーポレート事業統括　法人ビジネス事業部
バーチャル・セールスマネージャー
Virtual Sales Manager/
Corporate Business Supervisor
Corporate Business Division
●入社年　**Employed since**　　　2010

仕事のポリシー　　My work policy

滞らないことや効率性を第一に考え完璧を求めすぎないことで、複数のタスクをこなす。

Achieve multiple tasks by not pursuing completeness too much, but rather thinking to avoid jams and work effectively.

山田 晴香　Haruka Yamada

●部署と役職　**Section and position**
プロダクト マネージャー
テクニカル サービス
Product Manager
Technical Services
●入社年　**Employed since**　　　2004

シスコの好きなところ　　Why do you like Cisco?

Inclusion & Collaboration の浸透、個の強みを活かしつつお互い尊重し合える文化。

Wide-spread understanding of "Inclusion & Collaboration" and a corporate culture that fosters mutual respect and individual strengths.

［編者］

Project Quantum事務局

高橋 史子、山中 朋子、吉田 由華、山口 智愛、宮川 愛、平澤 典子

「Project Quantum」は、世界最大のコンピュータネットワーク機器開発会社、シスコシステムズの日本法人であるシスコシステムズ合同会社における女性リーダー育成のためのプロジェクトチーム。部門横断的に選抜された女性幹部候補生たちが、OJTやディスカッションを通じ、リーダーとしての資質を磨いていく、日本独自のプログラム。

リーダーをめざす貴女へ
——Discover the Aspiring Leader In You

2016年4月21日　第1刷発行

編　者	シスコシステムズ合同会社 Project Quantum事務局
発行所	**ダイヤモンド社** 〒150-8409　東京都渋谷区神宮前6-12-17 http://www.diamond.co.jp/ 電話／03·5778·7235（編集）　03·5778·7240（販売）
制作統括	宮﨑晃彦（株式会社北斗社）
編集制作進行	森恒三、大森香保子
編集	飯島愛、サクセスブック社
翻訳	シスコ翻訳チーム、サクセスブック社
装丁、本文デザイン・DTP	
	中嶋かをり（N&Iシステム コンサルティング 株式会社）、高野睦子
イラストレーション	CHIPS（CHIPS CLUB）
撮影	武井優美（株式会社スタジオアイランド）、関幸貴
製作進行	小野 幹朗（株式会社北斗社）、ダイヤモンド・グラフィック社
印刷	八光印刷(本文)・慶昌堂印刷(カバー)
製本	本間製本
編集担当	前田早章

©2016 シスコシステムズ合同会社
ISBN 978-4-478-06891-5
落丁・乱丁本はお手数ですが小社営業局宛にお送りください。送料小社負担にてお取替えい
たします。但し、古書店で購入されたものについてはお取替えできません。
無断転載・複製を禁ず
Printed in Japan